FROM THE TEMPLE TO THE POOL

Reflecting on the Journey, Reigniting Trust and Choosing to Move

TRINA MILLER

From the Temple to the Pool / Trina Miller
ISBN-13: 979-8-218-27890-8

This work is dedicated to the countless people who have walked with my family through the deepest and most profound seasons of life.

There are women who have inspired me, men who have challenged me, and friends who have walked closer than a brother. I wouldn't be here today without you.

CONTENTS

ACKNOWLEDGMENTS

To my amazing husband Ken and beautiful children, Josiah and Trinity—you have kept me going when everything within me wanted to give up. You have loved me through indescribable pain and given me a reason to press on. Words fail to describe the gratitude that overwhelms my heart when I reflect on how blessed I am to be the wife and mother to such incredible people.

And to my precious Jude, the magnetic, funny, and courageous little man who changed our family forever—you were a gift wrapped in perfection and loved profoundly from the time we all dreamed about the possibility of you. We cherish your memory and long for the day when we are together again.

Finally, to my Savior and Lord, Jesus—You have walked me through the fire, held me in the shadow of Your wing, and loved me without condition. This story is a testimony of Your goodness. Thank You for Your grace. Because of You, it is well with my soul.

CHOOSING YOUR HEALING

While He was passing by, He noticed a man [who had been] blind from birth. [2] His disciples asked Him, "Rabbi (Teacher), who sinned, this man or his parents, that he would be born blind?" [3] Jesus answered, "Neither this man nor his parents sinned, but it was so that the works of God might be displayed and illustrated in him."

—John 9:1–3

I n John 9, we read the story of a blind man sitting in his usual, everyday begging spot at the temple gate. Maybe his other senses had developed to be more acute because of his disability. I imagine his ears were keenly attuned to the activity around him. He was sitting at the entrance to the temple, which customarily was where those who could not go out and earn a living would loiter to receive sympathy, in the form of money or food, from passersby.

He heard a group of men walking by and talking about his "poor" condition. He listened to their conversation about what he or his parents must have done to earn him such a life of disappointment and suffering.

Consider what this situation must have felt like for the blind man. You may be imagining with me that something profound occurred in his mind. Likely, he had heard already of this man Jesus and those who were His followers. I wonder if he already had an opinion of Jesus and who He was.

The blind man probably knew that there had just been a colossal altercation between Jesus and His disciples, on the one hand, and the local religious leaders threatening to stone Him for blasphemy, on the other. Bible scholars tell us that the dispute likely happened in the Court of the Gentiles at the temple gate. Jesus, as always, kept His cool, addressed the fear most of us would have felt when hearing the truth, and kept moving. I wonder if the blind man had heard the commotion of that recent confrontation.

Now he heard the conversation about someone the disciples were passing, who must have committed some kind of offense to deserve his disability. Did he think, at first, they were talking about another blind man? I wonder how long it took him to figure out he was the subject of their exchange. And I wonder if he assumed, in his unbelieving heart, that there was something accurate in the disciples' assumption—

that his blindness was someone's fault.

In any case, I'm confident that when he realized they were talking about him, their words must have stung him deeply. Words have such power, especially when heard audibly from someone we regard as an authority. Those words hurt all the more when they seem to confirm the same whispers with which we've been contending inside our heart.

Many of us, when suffering, hear about our perceived disability from well-intentioned friends or acquaintances who want to diagnose or put a label on our pain. Their effort to explain away what we cannot may help them settle questions in their heart. After all, one of the main questions of mankind since the beginning of time is, *"Why?"*

Personally, I know I have a litany of *why* questions to ask God someday. Why do bad things happen to good people? Why, when we serve Him with all our heart, mind, soul, and strength, aren't we exempt from suffering? Why do we sometimes experience pain and suffering that redefine our life to the point we lose who we are and stumble off the path of favor and blessing, and into more pain instead?

Why do evil people prevail and have the blessings godly people intercede and beg for? When the rug is pulled out from under us, our effort to understand *why*, unfortunately, can lead us to put too much belief in the theories of those around us—especially if they appear to have everything together.

To take it a step further, what must this anonymous blind man have felt as he heard Jesus respond with the truth? As we know from Scripture, the truth breaks chains and brings freedom. Not that there isn't work we choose to embrace as we process truth into action, but I believe this man's heart leaped when he heard Jesus speak. Jesus hadn't yet spoken his name or addressed him directly, but He did speak truth into the man's pain. I believe just hearing the words bore witness in his soul, sparked hope within him, and set him free.

Suddenly, as his reality was shifting, he heard Jesus spit.

Did he think Jesus just needed to get something out of His mouth or had an overproduction of saliva? I can't imagine he knew what Jesus was up to. How often do you?

Next, he felt a touch on his eyes. It wasn't a love pat or a soothing "there, there," but an application of something on his eyes.

Think now of the legal requirement of a God-fearing Jew. If you touched a wound, it would make you unclean. I'm sure this man didn't get many loving touches as people passed him by while he sat outside begging. And I'm confident that the feeling of mud being applied to his eyes seemed even stranger, especially since he had just heard Jesus spit! Is anything much more offensive than getting spit on?

The increased darkness must have been confusing and possibly frightening. If you don't know what I'm talking about, put your hand over your closed eyes and notice that the darkness gets darker. This man was about to learn a valuable lesson in trusting God: more darkness does not mean God isn't in control.

I realize I'm paraphrasing a lot and making some assumptions about the blind man's situation. Still, I want you to understand that when we are faced with a problem or a story, we can fail to see it from the perspective of those living it.

That's what this book is all about—perspective in the midst of pain and triumph. Many people who read it, and even those who were part of it, will have different perspectives. This one is mine. My desire is that the stories you read will spark hope within you, challenge your thinking, and allow you to see that sometimes, even when the darkness gets darker, we are only a few steps away from our victory.

In this story, Jesus took something incredibly offensive, made a mud pie with it, and stuck it on the eyes of a man who couldn't see and begged for a living, without so much as acknowledging him directly. That sounds pretty rough when put in those terms.

However, if you choose to see it from a different perspective, Jesus was accomplishing a couple of things. First, he was correcting the theology of the day by ensuring this man heard the truth about his pain. Second, He created an amazing opportunity for this man to choose healing with his trust and obedience.

I hope that challenges you: *he chose his healing.* Jesus took what was offensive and then used His hands to combine it with dirt, the substance of our original creation. Dirt was what our Father lovingly collected with His hands to form us in His image, in our perfect state.

Jesus applied the offense, with the substance of our original intent, and then issued a call to obedience. His request that the man wash himself in the Pool of Siloam began a journey of trust, which this man chose to take without knowing the outcome. Jesus didn't tell him that if he went to the pool, his eyes would be open. He simply told him to go.

As you walk down the path of my personal journey, I wish I could say that the same blind faith this man demonstrated is what you will find. It's not. However, God in His amazing mercy has stuck by me through every hill and valley with the patience of a loving father. He has shown me that although I have grown personally under the shadow of His wing, I have not done anything amazing to get where I am today. In fact, my best performance is but filthy rags in His eyes. My overcoming has occurred solely because of the sacrifice Jesus made so that I could be covered in His righteousness and be made entirely whole. The very same is available to you!

PART ONE

THE SPIT

CHAPTER ONE

ABANDONMENT

Look to the right [the point of attack] and see;
For there is no one who has regard for me [to act in my favor].
Escape has failed me and I have nowhere to run;
No one cares about my life.

⁵ I cried out to You, O LORD;
I said, "You are my refuge,
My portion in the land of the living."

—Psalm 142:4–5

On a day in May with no particular significance (unless you happen to be Israeli), I was born in a place called Aberdeen, Washington. Aberdeen is a small logging and fishing community that, when I was young, bustled with millwork and all sorts of jobs coming in from all over Washington State.

That day, at the community hospital, I joined a family of three: my sister, who was five years older than me, and my parents, who had been married for seven years at the time. Unfortunately, by the time I was five, my parents decided to divorce after being married for twelve years. At five years old, I didn't understand that there were even problems. However, I remember that opportunities to spend time with my dad and have him around were limited at best. He was rarely home when my parents were married, and after they divorced, I only saw him a couple of times. When he was around, it was a blast, and I loved having him there. Yet, I didn't have any concept of what it was like to have a full-time dad in my life.

My sister was ten years old when the divorce happened. Like many her age, she struggled with the adjustment to life knowing her dad was gone. She had twice the memories of the family dynamics, both good and bad. At eleven, she needed a change of scenery and decided to run away from home. I remember feeling confused, but more than that, the reality that I was alone sunk in all the way to my bones. My six-year-old brain could not see her pain.

All I knew was that people kept leaving me and I hadn't seen any of it coming. I didn't understand yet, of course, that I would eventually have issues to work through from the departure of my dad. It wasn't until much later that I was able to recognize some of the burden I was carrying. Some of the emotional instability I fought in life stemmed from the timing of both my sister and my dad leaving so closely together.

A few years later, my mother married a gentleman for whom she had been working as a bookkeeper. He was a single dad with four boys (two at home) and was self-employed as a log truck driver. Her decision to marry him was not one I was pleased about. As an idealistic young kid, I felt strongly that her and my dad belonged together and would reconcile at some point. This man was definitely going to get in the way of that!

Additionally, he wasn't very nice; in fact, he was rather gruff and mean. He would often say horrible things to her, and rarely was he ever kind to me. Overall, I would say he was destructive in his behavior. I could not understand why she would want to marry him, and I felt that my happiness and security were far from her mind. Why I would ever be forced to call him Dad and pretend to be happy about this new, instant family was beyond me.

Added to that, I didn't understand why I wasn't allowed to visit my own dad anymore (not that there had been many opportunities before). I hated that horrible things were suddenly being said about him in our home. I only knew my dad as my hero, not as the person their words made him out to be. Life had shifted dramatically in the span of a few short years. I started to shrink back into a shell of expectations and people-pleasing.

About two years into their marriage, my family decided to make a move to a little town called Sequim, Washington. I, like any eleven-year-old, was devastated at the idea of leaving all of my family and friends. It wasn't long, however, before I fell in love with the adventure of a new place. Mostly, it birthed ideas in my imagination about what a family could be, and I began falling in love with dreams for the future.

During this time, we went to a small church. Though I had accepted the Lord as my Savior at a very young age, I was now beginning to develop a relationship with Him as my friend and constant companion. As my identity began developing through this companionship, I chose to get baptized and ul-timately started to have the first pings in my heart nudging me toward ministry—evangelism in particular.

For the first time, I got involved in my school, too. My first-ever effort to step out and ask for acceptance resulted in joining the drill team. Many things were starting to come to-gether in this new life I had outside of the home. Life was actually feeling stable for the first time since my dad left.

Especially in our little church, I truly felt I had an identity. Being a young pre-teen, I was attached to church as a place I felt I finally belonged. After feeling lost for as long as I could remember, I found that my church had become a sanctuary for my heart.

It was a small church led by a young family with whom I had begun to build a deep relationship over time. They had a son who was just a couple years younger than me and a three-year-old girl they had adopted after the loss of their daughter a few years earlier.

I was in love with this little family and the idea that family could exist the way I dreamed. I still remember vividly how I watched them interact and respond to one another in the most loving and supportive way I had ever seen. It sparked a yearning in my heart to have a family of my own someday who would love each other the way they did.

After only about a year and a half, my mom and stepdad decided that it was time to return to our original home in Aberdeen. It was the middle of the school year, and I was devastated at the decision to leave after overcoming the hurdle of not wanting to move in the first place. My mom reluctantly agreed that I could stay with our pastor friends for the remainder of the school year and then return to my family in the summertime, in about six months.

I was delighted to stay with this family! I dove head-first into their regular day-to-day activities, wanting to ensure I was a contributing member of the household. Here I was at twelve years old, terrified that if I was too much work for them or if I couldn't *do* enough to influence them to want me to stay, this dream life could be over.

I absolutely loved the dynamics of their home life. I loved having meals together where everybody laughed and enjoyed one another. And I also saw another side of this family, which solidified in my heart what love in the midst of pain looks like in the practicality of the day-to-day.

I mentioned that this beautiful family had lost their first daughter a couple of years before the adoption of their youngest. In the safety of their home, I saw them embrace the pain of their loss and love each other through the times of remembrance, which seemed to come often and out of nowhere. And during the expected, painful milestones like birthdays and anniversaries, they loved each other so purely, with no judgment, while allowing each other the space to grieve individually. I had a unique opportunity to view raw pain worked out through a lens of unconditional love while with this family.

At the same time, I saw what trust in a real and present God could help one overcome. Although I couldn't fathom what they were going through, I saw a bond in this family beyond just getting along and appearing to be all "Wonderbread" on the surface. I saw a deep-rooted trust in the Lord and a foundation I wanted to have in my life.

As expected, when the summer came, it was time to move back to Aberdeen and rejoin my own family. Although I begged and begged my mom to let me stay longer with this other family (forever if I could), my pleading was ineffective. I had no choice but to go. I look back on that situation now as a mother and wonder how devastating it must have been for my mom to have her child want to be in a different family.

My heart was not one of disrespect or lack of love for my mom. In fact, I clearly remember not wanting to cause her pain. My desire to stay was simply because of the love and security I felt by being part of the family I had grown to love. It wasn't a "better off" scenario in my mind. Instead, I experienced a deep compelling inside to never again be absent from this feeling of safety.

But this season also marked the beginning of a dream in my heart. Although I had grown incredibly attached to that beautiful family, when I left I took with me a newly birthed friendship with God. I had begun to talk with Him as my constant companion and share my heart with Him, and I relied on Him to be my strength as I walked through another separation. He was my best friend and would be with me wherever I went. The safety of His love would be exactly what I needed as I sprung headlong into adolescence.

REFLECTION

The concept of family is not one we come up with on our own. God has created us to be part of His family. We see all over Scripture the importance of belonging—of being part of something.

No doubt, one of the tragedies in broken families is learning to walk through the foregone conclusion that someone has left because we weren't enough to keep them there. The truth, however, is that God has promised never to leave us or forsake us. When we learn to find our security in Him instead of the people around us, our expectation changes. We can recognize that we are all broken people in one way or another. The security found in being part of God's family opens the door for us to release others who may have unintentionally hurt us due to their own pain. That release will lead to forgiveness if we let it. And forgiveness always paves the way to healing.

CHAPTER TWO

REJECTION AND HIDING

Come to Me, all who are weary and heavily burdened [by religious rituals that provide no peace], and I will give you rest [refreshing your souls with salvation].

—Matthew 11:28

I moved home just in time for school to start. Once again, I would be going to a new campus—and a middle school at that! We had moved into a small-town suburb of sorts called Central Park. My parents didn't want me to go to either of the two closest schools, and our little community didn't have a middle school available. That left me taking the city bus, which meant a quarter-mile walk, a ten-mile ride, and a bus transfer across town to Hoquiam High School. It would take about ninety minutes to complete the process, so I had to start about two hours before school.

I was accustomed to being on my own, and I had walked myself to and from school as young as six. I also had years of experience keeping myself occupied for hours while waiting for my mom to get home from work in the afternoon after my sister had left. Now I had stepbrothers around, and my mom had stopped working outside the home. She was at the house more often, including in the afternoons when I got home from school. Life had changed so much in the few years after my mom's remarriage, but the daily routine of the bus ride brought back some of those old memories.

Even though I resented that bus ride at the time, I look back on it now as a great gift. On those rides, I began recognizing a need for the Lord in my family life. I also began to pray as a daily habit. Some of my prayers focused on the creepy-seeming passengers, specifically that they would never talk to or sit next to me. Other prayers were focused on the boys I liked and wanted to pay me attention. But many were about who I would marry someday. I was thirteen, after all. Through those conversations with God, my spirit grew inside me, and my friendship with Him became more and more of a necessity for survival in the middle school season.

I didn't have deep relationships with anyone. I was part of the family at home but also somewhat withdrawn emotionally, instead of being fully immersed. As a means to protect myself from getting hurt, I found that I was beginning to develop unhealthy self-reliance, with a whopping dose of determination to be different than what I saw around me. It was easier (or safer) for no one to know that I was less than perfect. I was never bad, disrespectful, disobedient, or rebellious—when anyone was looking, anyway. When I misbehaved or did things I knew were wrong, I found it easier to punish myself than to allow anyone to know I was capable of less than perfection.

Talk about a head case: I knew I needed punishment, so I just did it myself! Understanding the cause and effect necessary for me to experience consequences for my actions somehow had gotten in my DNA. (It was probably the one time I remember my dad ever spanking me.) But disciplining myself over those consequences when they needed to occur was a whole different animal.

I'm not writing about this to celebrate my behavior at all. Quite the opposite, actually. I want you to understand how deep my need to stay hidden and perfect in everyone's sight had already become at such a young age. Naturally, after a few groundings and missed nights of television, I figured out that if I didn't misbehave, I wouldn't feel the compulsion to experience the discipline. I had heard a sermon about putting on the armor of God, and since I spent time talking to God daily, I could just add this prayer into the routine and would never struggle with the traps of the enemy. Ah, naivety.

My young heart was already beginning to hide behind the performance of religion. My prayers were becoming a formula, and my friendship with God was becoming all about my wants and needs. It was simply a superficial means to get my way, as if God were a cosmic genie in the sky.

Being a dreamer at heart, and with the idea that I now had God wrapped around my little finger, I shifted away from the simple dream of my earlier years for love, safety, and security—I was *so* juvenile back then, I thought—to much bigger aspirations. I dreamed about being Miss America someday. I dreamed about fame, fortune, revenge, and greater perfection. If everyone loved me and wanted to be just like me, I would have proved my worth externally. (It's embarrassing to write all this, folks!)

That said, it wasn't all so shallow. I also dreamed about being a mother, a wife, and a positive influence. We had some close friends who were traveling evangelists, and I was convinced that I would travel the world and sing songs to the Lord. I would inspire people to surrender everything to God and devote their lives fully and entirely to Him.

I was sure I would marry into that very family one day. One of my earliest heartbreaks came from an utterly unintentional expectation from my parents and these evangelist friends of ours to marry me off to the family's youngest son. Though I was all on board and seeing myself riding off into the sunset with him, he went and married someone else. How dare he? I don't know how on earth I had gotten so invested in this vision, but I was fully bought in and convinced it was my destiny.

In fairness to my dreaming, it wasn't all in my head. He was my first kiss (behind the church after revival service, no less). He would also pass notes to me during service, directing me to very seductive Song of Solomon scriptures. What I failed to recognize, though, was that he was not genuinely into me. He had many other towns to pass through, many more opportunities to kiss girls behind churches, and zero interest in being an evangelist.

I was confident, though, that his lack of response to my countless long-distance letters, and lack of any effort toward a relationship, was somehow my fault. I wasn't good enough for him, and I knew it; worse yet, he knew it. Thus, the birth of fundamental rejection. This "not good enough" mindset wasn't new. In fact, it was foundational for me. As it grew more debilitating, it made my resolve to be perfect even greater.

Several years before, there had been an occasion when I mistakenly allowed one of my private dreams to be known. On my eleventh birthday, when my mom and I went to get my ears pierced (because was finally allowed), I let my guard down: I told my mom I wanted to be Miss America when I grew up.

Though American Idol didn't exist yet, as a little girl I watched and imitated the Mandrell sisters. I just knew I was destined to sing on a stage while receiving a crown, as the world looked on and agreed that I was to be admired!

When I let this dream slip out, my mom looked at me and said, with a bit of loving sarcasm, "Whatever you want, honey." I perceived her desire not to see me disappointed as doubt in my ability to achieve my dream. As a result, I determined that I would only practice in private. Then, someday, I would emerge out of nowhere, ready to wow everyone around me!

One night, while practicing a song in my room, I bellowed a powerful rendition of Carmen's "Fear Not My Child" at the top of my lungs. I was confident my singing was getting stronger by the day. But when I got called down for dinner shortly after, to my horror, my stepdad said, "It sounds like you're wounding an animal up there."

While I'm sure he thought he was funny, I was crushed and embarrassed. Now they knew about my heart's desire and were poking fun at my ability. They didn't believe I was capable. In response, I internalized my stepdad's comment and let my passion fuel my resolve to take control. At the same time, though, I began to develop an enormous fear of what other people thought of me and what they would think if they, too, knew the deep part of my heart where my dreams lived.

The need to shelter myself emotionally from anybody knowing I was capable of doing something wrong now had an added layer of secrecy around it. I didn't want anyone to know what I held in my heart. Naturally, if they did, they wouldn't believe my dreams were possible, either, or that I was good enough to achieve them. I already knew I couldn't handle people's responses, but I also knew I needed development to be excellent. The natural and easy solution was to push myself without anyone knowing.

Internally, I knew I was capable and believed that the impossible was available for me. I was confident in that, and in who I belonged to. With my whole being, I knew that God was a good Father and had amazing things in store for my life. I would pursue my dreams, and I would get what I wanted. Though I would be relentless about it, nobody else needed to know.

Despite my determination to hide myself and to withdraw the reality of who I was on the inside, like many young girls I was blessed with one friend who knew everything. Kristen and I had been inseparable since we were five years old. Our parents were in a Christian band together, and just to spend time together, we never missed a practice or a performance. We each knew the other's darkest and most profound secrets. She was a God-given sister who became my living, breathing diary.

Kristen was the one who believed I could be, or do, anything I put my mind to. She championed my talents and encouraged my dreams. Kristen didn't make me feel small or insignificant for having them, either. She kept me going to youth group and singing in the choir, and she fueled a tiny flicker of hope that my heart could be safe in the right hands.

The summer before our first year in high school, we got to participate in a community youth event. All the churches in our area had gotten together and planned a back-to-school Beach Bum Bash for all the high-school-aged kids in our local area. We stayed a few nights in one of the church buildings, holding services throughout the day and spending evenings around the fire. The services were impactful; they were meant to help us dig deeper in Christ before we faced the impending school year and its distractions. Kristen and I both recommitted our lives to the Lord. We were inspired to evangelize the hallways of our school with weekly prayer groups and by doing worship together with other kids from our area.

On the last night of the event, I had one of those deeply inspired dreaming moments where I was overcome with expectation. God had filled my heart. I was excited about the year to come and was anticipating big things for my future. Then, as I watched the band on the stage, I couldn't help but be drawn to the (very cute!) drummer. He had a spirit about him as he played that I had never seen in a boy before. The presence of God seemed tangible on him, and there was a tenderness in his eyes that captured my attention. I couldn't look away.

When we prayed just before the last song of the night, I whispered to Kristen, "I'm going to marry him." She looked up at me and giggled. Then we both bowed our heads and went to the last beach fire of the event, without another word about this mystery drummer.

Deep inside, though, a "how do you like me now?" theology was taking root. On the one hand, I was developing a deep passion for inspiring people. I wanted to show people not only who I could be but also how living a life of purpose, serving God, and loving each other could be incredibly fulfilling. On the other hand, I was nurturing a selfish desire to be admired for my capability, hiding my heart in fear of the pain of rejection. I stopped fully sharing my heart with Kristen.

Unfortunately, this other path would send me on a *very* long walk down the "temple staircase" to the pool of healing—tripping and flailing all the way because I couldn't see clearly. Like the blind man Jesus sent to Siloam, I had eyes covered with offense.

REFLECTION

The story of the blind man creates many questions in my mind. I know that in our humanity, we bear such questions, especially when faced with offenses that pile up like mud on our eyes. Those offenses can feel like darkness overtaking us.

When we have been struggling to find hope in the most difficult of circumstances, offenses can build up, layer by layer, and threaten our ability ever to see clearly.

A bigger problem with offenses is that they can isolate us and lead us to put a shield around our heart. As cliché as it may sound, the truth is that we are born into a broken and sinful world. Some of us seemingly have everything handed to us. In contrast, others struggle physically, emotionally, and mentally with issues we've done nothing to bring on ourselves.

Layer onto this the fact that many people born into especially difficult circumstances face life challenges more intense or extensive than you or I may ever confront. Maybe these are bigger challenges, or maybe the piling on of the mud just makes things so dark that the person gets stuck.

Whatever you may have faced in life, or whatever you may have seen others face, the truth is that nothing can separate us from the love of God. His heart is for us to see clearly and be restored to His original intent for us—to never be separated from Him.

Take a moment and reflect on the times in your life when things seemed to pile on, one after another. Did you feel like there was something you must have done to deserve such difficulty? How did God reveal the truth to you in those moments?

On the flip side, do you feel like you have lived a good life and don't deserve to encounter difficulty? In reality, whether we think we deserve it or were born into undeserved difficulty, there is nothing that can separate us from the love of God. He always has a plan to redeem, heal, and restore us.

CHAPTER THREE

SELF-RELIANCE AND CONTROL

Not that we are sufficiently qualified in ourselves to claim anything as coming from us, but our sufficiency and qualifications come from God.

—2 Corinthians 3:5

Much to my surprise and delight, my sister moved back to our little town during the summer before my sophomore year in high school. She had gotten married and now had two beautiful little girls I was crazy about! I loved having her around, and I loved getting to be an auntie.

As always before, my sister was on a pedestal in my eyes. I was proud she was my sister, and I wanted to be just like her. Our relationship was pretty distant, though. We were very different, or so we thought, and didn't know each other well. I had hurt in my heart from her leaving me, while she had devastating amounts of hurt in her life over what she had experienced while growing up in a series of environments not meant for anyone to thrive in. Her background was significantly different from what I had known as a child. Still, the manifestation internally was much the same for us both.

She and her husband were looking to start a new life back in our town when they came to live with their girls. I couldn't have been more excited that they were close! Unfortunately, my expectation soon became disappointment when we weren't besties right out of the gate. A lot of water had passed under the bridge for both of us, leaving us in two substantially different stages of life.

As the school year started, I felt the need to make some money and step into the workforce. I heard about a drive-in, in town, that would hire at fifteen-and-a-half with a work permit. I went there one day, and Denna, my good friend for several years, happened to be working at the counter on the afternoon shift. Naturally, I thought it would be a great place to fit in and get some experience working in the "real world." Being able to do it with a friend was just icing on the cake! Denna was willing to give me a reference, so I was hired and began working a handful of hours after school a few days a week.

Much to my delight, I immediately discovered that the incredibly handsome fry cook was the drummer from the Beach Bum Bash that Kristen and I had attended just a few months prior. I was still just as enamored with him the day I discovered him at work as I had been watching him drum in worship at the concert.

I could hardly act normal in his presence, though I wasn't in his company much. We didn't work closely together, but we literally crossed paths as his shift ended and mine began. I felt like a bumbling idiot every time I tried to look cool when he would pass by, or wrestled with essential words whenever he tried to say a polite hello. I couldn't help but be distracted when he left work and stood outside for several minutes, next to his car, to talk with his friends before they went their separate ways. I would stand by the window and pretend to make milkshakes, or grab something I pretended a customer wanted, so I could admire him from a distance and dream about what he must be like.

I had this admiration for him, yet he hardly knew I existed. He certainly never would have guessed what was going on deeper inside me as I grew desperate to take control and change my environment at home. I was at the height of my difficult years as a teen, balancing my love and desire to serve God with a "fight or flight" impulse to take matters into my own hands. I couldn't stand being told what to do anymore. I couldn't stand the harsh words, and I couldn't believe that my dad really didn't want me. I needed him desperately, so I resolved to prove to him that he needed me, too. From my limited vantage point, living with my dad had translated into a perfect, "white picket fence" kind life for my sister. I thought that must be what I needed as well.

I had admired everything about my sister for as long as I could remember. She was brave, resilient, and courageous enough to run away and put herself in a better situation. Why couldn't I do the same? I contemplated numerous scenarios that would put me in a better position, too.

Ultimately, I decided to borrow forty dollars from a friend so I could have fare from my local bus station in Aberdeen, Washington, to Portland, Oregon. I would show up on my dad's doorstep and change both of our lives for the better. I just knew he would be delighted to have me! I could see the reunion in my head. When dreaming, I could hear the stories of his failed attempts to be in my life. I knew it would be challenging to accomplish, yet I was convinced that if I could simply get to him, everything was going to be alright—even blissful.

Clearly, the dangerous realities of overnight public transportation, complete with filthy stops in shady stations to change buses, didn't factor into my dreams. What I saw and experienced in the eight hours it took me to get to Portland was an education in what truly troubled kids experience. This revelation of my naivety should have been a warning to me, but I was so fixated on the goal, I could see no alternatives.

During the final stop before reaching Portland, I worked up the courage to call my dad from a payphone to tell him I would be arriving at the downtown bus station within a few hours. He was shocked but agreed to pick me up that morning. Of course, I didn't give him much choice, but I was euphoric nonetheless. I had done it! Operation Great Life could now begin.

More than the need to escape from life in Washington, or my dream of the perfect family life, I had a driving desire to connect with my dad. I had seen him maybe three or four times since the day, ten years before, when he told me he wouldn't be coming home. I desperately wanted a relationship with him, and I was sure that the only reason he wasn't around was because my mom and stepdad were keeping him from me somehow. I was looking for safety, and I needed love without condition. I was determined to find all the missing pieces in my life by taking control and making things happen myself.

I loved getting to know my dad, who is tender-hearted and warm—truly a wonderful man. Unfortunately, he was also ill-equipped to be a dad. I immediately found that what was important to me, including what I needed for support in my day-to-day activities, simply wasn't available.

I didn't know at the time that my dad was one of thirteen children and had grown up in an extremely abusive environment. He left home at twelve and joined the circus because they would take minors. When not with the circus, he traveled all over the country and wound up on the streets, fending for himself as a very young man. Eventually, he made his way out west and into a program called Teen Challenge, where he would be introduced to a Savior who loved him completely and would give him a family.

It's taken many years for me to understand that based on how my dad grew up, though his love and commitment to my sister and me might not have met our expectations, they were far above what he had experienced in his upbringing. In any case, at the time, I was looking for something I wasn't going to get from him.

My spiritual reflexes kicked in and compelled me to get plugged into a youth group. I had enough foundation to know that I needed the Lord. Despite my obvious rebellion against my mom and stepdad, I knew He would allow me to hide under the shadow of His wing in my disappointment.

I began to write apologetic letters to my mom, expressing how sorry I was for the horrible worry she must have been experienced not knowing where I was or if I was okay. Back in those days, there were no cell phones or emails, just landlines (which had long-distance charges) and snail mail. I hoped she had figured it out. To this day, I still don't know for sure how the discovery of my disappearance affected her. I do remember not wanting to hurt her, and I hoped that she understood where I was emotionally. I wrote her those letters of apology with a pure heart, with the intent of not having her blame herself for my choice.

While tending to the matter of trying to make things right with my mom, I was also trying my best to adjust to life in a new place, with new people. I quickly stuffed my dashed hopes for the perfect father–daughter reunion deep in my soul. Once again, I found myself in a situation of self-reliance and survival. In my mind, if I was going to turn this decision to move to Oregon into a good one, I needed to take control and make it work.

Naturally, part of making it work would be the ability to support myself. So I got a job and started earning my own keep, paying all my expenses (except a place to sleep). Deep inside, I thought that if I could avoid being a burden, perhaps I could earn the affection I so desired.

My dad was present physically but not emotionally. My stepmom was consumed with ensuring that my presence didn't interrupt her and her son's world. She was ostensibly okay with my company as long as she completely controlled my father's affection. Before long, it became no mystery to me that she was less than thrilled I was there to stay long-term. It seemed as if my attempt at finding a place in my dad's heart would be out of the question if she had anything to do with it.

It wasn't that my needs were so great, mind you, and I was determined not to be a drag on anyone's energy bank. I believe she was concerned about how her life might change if my dad shared his heart. Years later, I would come to understand that her fear of rejection manifested in rejection of me. For the moment, I did my best to stay involved in church and separate myself from the family life I wanted so bad. It was easier and less painful just to keep busy.

As I began to be completely consumed with my job, the number of hours I was putting in became significant. I was finding success and personal satisfaction in my work life. In fact, it was liberating to realize that if I did my best, I could earn the attention and affection of my leaders and receive the accolades I was desperate to hear at home.

Though I was only sixteen years old, I was quickly recognized as a leader at the McDonald's restaurant where I worked. I prided myself on never staying still. If I wasn't wooing a customer with all my charm, I was cleaning something and making it look brand-new. I committed myself to having the best service times of anyone in the restaurant. If there was going to be a comment card submitted about any employee, I was determined it would be me!

The restaurant I worked at, in Milwaukie, Oregon, was about to become the first twenty-four-hour McDonald's in the state. We were going to test the concept for other franchises and see if we could grow revenue using a cross-trained skeleton team to handle all the responsibilities with the equivalent efficiency of a full crew. A successful team needed highly self-motivated and responsible members to uphold standards while our regular leadership team slept through the night. I quickly volunteered, knowing that all eyes would be on this inaugural group.

I didn't understand how the labor laws worked back then; maybe my dad had to sign to let me do this (I don't remember). One way or another, here I was at sixteen years old, working a full-time job on the graveyard shift. Honestly, I don't think I asked permission, and I doubt my dad was concerned about me being gone all night long. I'm sure I wouldn't have taken no for an answer, anyway, if he had pushed back. I was wholly consumed and determined that nothing would get in the way of my success.

It wasn't long before my determination to shine was recognized further as a gift in leadership capability. Finding management for a graveyard shift at a fast-food restaurant couldn't have been easy, so it seemed natural to the store owners that I run the team. However, since I was under eighteen, I could not be promoted officially to a manager role. So my bosses formulated a unique management training program called the A-team, which allowed me to run a shift independently. The 11 p.m. to 7 a.m. Thursday to Tuesday team became mine, and my job was to make that drive-through the example from which all others would learn.

Naturally, I was excited about the opportunity to prove what I could do. I knew that if I could get everything working perfectly, my bosses would love me and further validate my drive toward perfection.

I didn't forget that I needed to finish high school; not graduating wasn't an option. Accordingly, I made sure I left in time to get to school by 8 a.m. Still, the work bug had bitten me hard, and I got a second job working three days a week at a tanning salon after school. Off work at McDonald's by 7 a.m., I made it to school by 8 a.m., was out at 2:30 p.m., and got to the tanning salon by 3 p.m. I left that job at 6 p.m. and had a short four hours to sleep before my shift at McDonald's started. Busying myself with making money, earning my keep, and staying out of everyone's way became a welcome escape from my emotions.

Eventually, I met an older man who was a regular at my restaurant. He would come by multiple times throughout the week and shower me with the compliments I strived so hard to earn. It wasn't long before I was completely enamored by him and by all the attention he was willing to give me. In those early days of our dating relationship, there wasn't a thing about him that didn't amaze me. He was seven years older, out of high school and college, and on to a career as an electrical lineman. He was established in life, with his own apartment, and was clearly successful—because he had a cell phone!

Here I was at sixteen years old, emotionally malnourished and utterly enamored with this man I had no business dating. I clearly needed the attention he was giving me. More than that, he represented the next level of proving my worth to the world around me: if I could have the love and affection of an older, good-looking, successful man who could easily date anyone he wanted, it would prove to everyone that I was worthy. My internal, "how do you like me now?" drive had kicked in on a grander scale, and in a much more dangerous way.

Never before had I felt so valuable; never before had I received the type of attention he gave me. I had a voice, and he listened. I had a presence he wanted to be near. And most of all, I wasn't too much effort for him. After all, he was the one pursuing me!

As our relationship grew, I was convinced I would marry this man and spend the rest of my life being adored by him. Suddenly, all the conditions I had placed on my future mate to be a Christ-loving, people-serving man went out the window. Of course, I believed I would eventually sway him to come to church with me, where he would (naturally) give his life to Jesus so we could serve in the church as a couple. That was enough justification for my decision to give in to him physically. After all, we were going to get married someday ... right?

About nine or so months into our relationship, in the spring of my junior year of high school, he disappeared. He wouldn't pick up the phone when I called, wouldn't answer the door when I came by his house, and stopped coming to see me at work. One day, two days, three days, and then a week went by with no answers—only confusion, pain, and utter devastation. I didn't understand what I had done wrong. It had to be something I did, though. Why else would he change his mind about me? This level of rejection cut deeper than I thought possible. I had believed he loved me, wanted me, and would never leave.

After a couple more weeks, a good friend of mine, who had also become his friend, finally rallied the courage to let me know he had found someone else. If the devastation were not unbearable enough already, the thought that I had been betrayed because someone better had come along was debilitating. No words could describe the emotion that racked my brain and my body as the truth began to set in. I had lost. I wasn't loved like I thought, and worst of all, now I was damaged goods.

I began to resolve, more than ever before, that I didn't need anybody. I could do life on my own. I could control my environment and my destiny. Everything going forward would be on my terms. I continued to pour myself, more and more, into work. As I did, I withdrew emotionally, not allowing any weakness or vulnerability to be known or seen even by those closest to me.

REFLECTION

From the beginning of time in the Garden of Eden to to-day, humanity has struggled with taking the reins from God to control our own destiny. While we've been given free will, His heart and desire for us are to rely on Him entirely. But in my experience, giving Him our wants is much easier than giving Him our pain, disappointment, and secret dreams.

It's probably safe to say that we have all experienced the pain of rejection in one way or another. The vicious cycle of lies that develops in our minds as a result is where the enemy runs rampant, overtaking our thoughts in an endless trap of self-pity and self-loathing. Those lies may have led you toward self-help and control as your defense.

The Bible refers to our need to wash our minds with the water of the Word (Ephesians 5:26). When we look to the Word for our truth, we find a supernatural comfort that paves the way toward deeper trust in a Father who doesn't change His mind about us. Building that confidence in Him enables us to relinquish control.

Trust will be a continuous theme in the pages of this book. Remember that trust is a process. Often within that process, I have failed to recognize that God has proved Himself repeatedly through the ages. Certainly, He has done so in my life! The trust journey is one hundred percent mine. It's a journey toward letting go of my grip on things, one teardrop at a time. This process has been painstakingly fruitful and ful-filling, as I believe it will be for you.

CHAPTER FOUR

PERFORMANCE

For it is by grace [God's remarkable compassion and favor drawing you to Christ] that you have been saved [actually delivered from judgment and given eternal life] through faith. And this [salvation] is not of yourselves [not through your own effort], but it is the [undeserved, gracious] gift of God; [9] not as a result of [your] works [nor your attempts to keep the Law], so that no one will [be able to] boast or take credit in any way [for his salvation]. [10] For we are His workmanship [His own master work, a work of art], created in Christ Jesus [reborn from above—spiritually transformed, renewed, ready to be used] for good works, which God prepared [for us] beforehand [taking paths which He set], so that we would walk in them [living the good life which He prearranged and made ready for us].

—Ephesians 2:8–10

A s I withdrew more and more at work, school, and church, I also began to look for the opportunity to start my path toward becoming Miss America. I know now that my focus was driven by a need to find approval. I was desperate to prove my worth to the world around me by showing how well I could perform and measure up to "their" (whoever *they* were) expectations of perfection. I could also prove that the man who devastated my heart would be sorry he let me go. Unfortunately, the realization of my true motivation would only come after many painful years of walking from one trap to another, while looking for that approval in all the wrong places.

Eventually, I found an advertisement for the Miss Teen Portland Pageant. What a perfect opportunity for me to get some pageant experience! I didn't want anybody to know I was interested. Heaven forbid I let anyone see that I had a dream in my heart.

Part of what I was experiencing was the still-burning question of why my boyfriend had rejected me in such a big way. I assumed something I did had run him off. Was I not pretty enough? Not thin enough? Not fun enough? Too much effort? Clearly, it must have been for a reason he didn't have the courage to tell me about. I determined to control my circumstances by beginning to control my future.

Over the course of the next few months, I wasted away to about one hundred pounds and became an absolute maniac about exercising. Food was now all I thought about: what foods I put in my mouth, or didn't; how often I ate and how many calories I was consuming. It was endless. In fact, I was convinced that the wait staff in restaurants who might see me as too thin would secretly put extra additives in my food and cause me to gain weight.

I was also utterly hyper-focused on becoming Miss Teen Portland. My new look would help me prove to everyone that I was valuable in somebody's eyes. They would see me as valuable enough to give me a title and recognize me publicly for all of the potential I had within me. Even as I write this, it sounds so self-centered, but the reality was that I needed acceptance. I needed validation from others to convince myself that there was value within me.

As I entered the program, I forgot a few important details. The biggest was the amount of money it was going to cost. My determination to succeed ultimately won out; however, I had to find a solution when I realized there was no way I would have the funds to complete the entrance requirement. Also, not to mention, I needed an evening gown, sportswear, and an interview suit. I would have to raise the money creatively.

I began to appeal to local businesses in the area by going door to door, seeking sponsorship. Before I knew it, I had not only paid the registration fee, but I also had gotten sponsors for every outfit. I would have to return them after and ensure the sponsoring businesses were named in the program, but that seemed like a small requirement for such generosity.

I was still working hard to ensure that my appearance was perfect, that I upheld my obligations at work, and that I earned perfect grades at school. Somehow, in all this, I learned the necessary walking techniques for the stage and practiced my talent until there was no opportunity for error.

The day of the pageant came before I knew it. The day itself started with a twelve-minute interview, before I spent the afternoon preparing for the evening show. The dressing rooms were filled with hairdressers, makeup artists, and overbearing mothers. By late afternoon, the emotional roller coaster the pressure brought on was evidenced in tears, frustration, and a ton of commotion. At my station, I did my own hair, makeup, and vocal warmups while watching the chaos around me.

Secretly, I wished someone were there to reassure me that even if I didn't win, I was a winner to them. I did wind up inviting one friend from work, after my dad and stepmother told me they weren't going to make it. I was so glad I did. She made it to the show and brought a couple of her friends, so I would have someone to greet at the reception afterward.

That night, as I stood on the stage, I discovered the magic of performing. My efforts toward perfection were paying off, and the applause I experienced fed a need deep inside. Since I knew only three people in that giant auditorium were there to support me, the cheers of the crowd were clear evidence that I had won them all over. I had never experienced such exhilaration in my life! It felt amazing to have people acknowledge publicly that my performances were better than the rest.

As the night wrapped up. I reflected on my entrance interview just a few months earlier. The applicant pool had started at about 1,500 girls. At first, I wasn't confident I would get in, but when I interviewed with the staff, the interest was evident on their faces. When I received the call that I had been selected, the competitor in me rose up in a way I hadn't seen coming. Obviously, it drove me to find those needed sponsors. On this night, it drove me to perform at my best as a way to win over the crowd and those judges.

As my name was called for the first runner-up title, I was disappointed in the defeat but inspired by the spark I felt inside. That spark would set a fire in me for performing. I could project whatever image of myself I wanted on a stage and nobody could say anything about it. No matter what anybody else in my life thought, I learned, I could go out and prove my ability to strangers. They would validate my need with their approval.

That moment was a vital decision point. It wasn't intentional, but a secret decision deep within that I didn't need God. I would have never said as much out loud, but in my heart, I felt I was getting better outcomes from my own effort than I was from prayer. My words seemed only to fall on deaf ears. In reality, the separation from the Lord probably began much earlier than this defining moment. Nonetheless, it was an unintentional turning point.

As the rift in my relationship with Him widened, I began doing things I had sworn I would never do. I started experimenting with alcohol, going to parties where I had no business, and numbingly giving myself to the boys who would pay me attention. I wasn't really thinking; instead, I chose to be hollow. I wouldn't let myself feel. Strangely, it was like walking around in someone else's body.

Although I was numb to the feelings my choices were creating at the time, I was driven by the illusion of control. I felt that my destiny was entirely in my own hands. In a sense, this was because I was choosing a side—one I had never been on before. It was a side that had more consequence than it had victory and more conditional love than unconditional love. Ultimately, it would lead to destruction.

I may have been in control, but I was also being controlled. I was controlled by that drive and determination to do life on my own terms. These terms included that I would never share my true heart or let my inadequacies ever be revealed. I was like an actress playing a character, and I alone got to define who that character would be. I was determined to perform in a way that fully embodied the things I wanted others to see. I wanted to be known by the superficial and be envied by the masses. I would show them! All those who cast me aside, counted me out, or defined me as unworthy would be put to shame. But it was a complete farce, and a setup for further destruction and hurt when the layers of masks eventually started to slip. Meanwhile, the emptiness inside only grew more profound.

Fortunately, because my relationship with the Lord had been so well established at a young age, it didn't take a lifetime to recognize how far away I had gotten from my first love. However, there were many painful years to come, first, before that reality set in fully. I didn't acknowledge for a long time how many of the developing consequences my choices had brought about.

One of the first revelations that rattled me to the core, as the effects of my drifting came into focus, was that I had an eating disorder. My dramatic weight loss might have been triggered by the sadness of my lost relationship, but it had grown into much more than that over time. I had developed a fear of eating certain items, worked out to exhaustion regularly, and was completely paranoid that anyone thinking I was too thin would sabotage me by sneaking "fattening" ingredients into my food.

The saddest part of this reality was, I didn't care that the issue had become severe. I actually liked having control. Sure, I assumed people wondered what I was doing to myself. Still, since I wasn't forcing myself to vomit or harming anyone else in the process, I felt no obligation or desire to discuss it with anyone. On the contrary, I preferred that people think I just had one of those enviable metabolisms that allowed me to eat whatever I wanted and never gain an ounce. Wasn't I lucky to have escaped the family curse? It was just the way I liked it: truth hidden by a chosen narrative, which I controlled.

Yet, as the initial clues continued to surface in my life, I was forced to see how far I had drifted from the choices I had vowed to God that I would keep. The broken promises were starting to stack up. I wouldn't be able to hide my lack of perfection for long. I had to do something, so I decided that it was time to go home to Washington. I figured it would be easier to re-center myself there, with all the friends and family I had left abruptly in the night a few years before.

In my mind, this transition should be simple. I had gained control of things that seemed out of my control. All I needed to do now was get back on track with my God. What better way to do that than to put myself in an environment where I hadn't struggled with the same issues I was running into in Portland? It seemed logical to me! So, the summer before my senior year in high school, I packed up the little car I had purchased (thanks to the help of a lovely couple in my church) with all the possessions I owned in the world and began the drive back to Washington.

As I drove the three hours by myself, there was a lot to think about that I couldn't run away from. My move was fueled by fear. I was afraid my life would go down a road I couldn't reverse. I didn't want to hurt my Father God by disappointing Him. Besides, I had seen many others on a crash course toward destruction with the same choices I was making. I was determined to not have that happen to me and figured that if I got in front of it now, I could change the outcome before anyone discovered that I needed help. There was one thing still hanging over my head, though: would my mom, whom I hurt so badly, welcome me back?

I rolled into Aberdeen late in the afternoon, anxious and unsettled, as I navigated to my sister's house and hoped she would be happy to see me. Fortunately, she was home and, though surprised I was there, let me use the phone to call my mom. Just before I dialed, she let me know that after I had left, my mom and stepdad got rid of all their belongings and bought a travel trailer. They permanently parked it in the yard of my grandparent's home in Copalis Crossing, Washington, which was about a twenty-five-minute drive from the high school I would attend.

Though unsure how I would fit into that scene, I quickly determined it was too late to second-guess and figured I'd better move forward fearlessly—but also with a *lot* of humility. So, I did it: I called and asked if I could come home. It was humiliating to admit I was wrong to leave, but in my mind, it was still way better than revealing the truth about why I needed to come home.

By God's mercy, I didn't need to try to fit into their ten-foot living space. Instead, my grandparents invited me to stay in the house with them. That was the open door I needed! Now I could just focus on getting back into an environment where I felt I could control who I was becoming. Then, all would be okay.

Unfortunately, I wasn't prepared for what I was about to encounter. Control is such an illusion—especially when your heart isn't in the right place. I thought that everything would naturally click when I returned to school. I would have the same friends, be involved in the same church, and so on. I was missing one minor detail, though: I wasn't the same person I was when I left, nor was anybody else. In fact, I had become a very different person than everyone had known before, and I couldn't hide it.

Almost immediately, my friends noticed the changes within me. Those who weren't still hurt and angry over my abrupt departure began to give me a lot of attention. Mind you, I had never been popular at school. I was your average, middle of the road goody-goody whom everyone liked but didn't necessarily think about having around at fun events. Now, though, all the boys I had swooned over my first year noticed me. I was getting invited to everything, and my physical changes seemed to place me in high demand.

The result of that attention simply revealed the true condition of my heart, as I began to slip right back into the same things I had got involved in back in Portland. I gave into that attention without hesitation, because I craved it so desperately. Any boys who showed me attention validated how wrong my boyfriend was to leave me, so I gave into their interest. I was careful not to disappoint anyone, to avoid giving them cause not to like me. I gave into the drinking and the parties and whatever I needed to do to ensure that I stayed in a relationship with the "right" people—those who would continue to shower me with attention. My need for approval was a brutal master.

At the end of my senior year, a dear evangelist friend of ours from when I was a kid—the one whose son I was convinced I would marry—came into town doing revival services. He set up nightly at a local church for the week. I decided to try to find a time to visit the family one night after work. I wasn't hungering for God in any way. Honestly, I was so full of indulgent pride that I wanted to show them how I had changed for the better. I was convinced they, too, would affirm my newfound perfection and shower me with accolades. I just knew they would tell me what a beautiful young woman I had blossomed into, and how they were so sad I wasn't their daughter-in-law. I was going to revel in their regret at dismissing my potential.

I arrived late to the service that evening and sat in the back. As I sat there, I was the one filled with regret. Almost immediately, the Holy Spirit began to move on my heart. I suddenly didn't care about the impression I would give, but I was sickened by the reality of the things I carried within me. The recognition of how far my relationship with the Lord had drifted smacked me in the face again. I had run from it, but the reality was still on my heels. How far I had gone past all of the things I swore I would never do and the relationships I swore I would never have! I had even failed at returning to the place of comfort and peace I had known before my big, bold move to Oregon. The environment I was in didn't return me to being the young Christ-follower I had longed to become again.

I was so disappointed in myself that the environmental change didn't get me back in spiritual shape. I had come into the meeting with such pride and couldn't wait to be recognized, but now, at this moment, the shame was suddenly unbearable. I wanted to hide. I now hoped they would have no idea who I was, since escaping out the back was going to be impossible.

The real problem was coming to the surface. My heart hadn't changed just because my environment did. I was still looking for validation from everyone else instead of seeking it from the Lord. I was hurt, rejected, angry, and abandoned (God's specialty!). I had sought the remedy on my own instead of running to a loving Father who would take all that pain on Himself and redeem it with blessings I could never earn.

As I sat in service fighting waves of despair, the Holy Spirit began to soften my heart. I was so profoundly convicted, so deeply grieved, and incredibly lost. There was no way for me to return. After all, God must be extremely disappointed in me. He, like so many before—my stepdad, my mom, my dad, my sister, my boyfriend—would reject me and not want anything to do with me. I wouldn't blame Him. I had been so foolish.

At the end of service, it was time for the altar call. I knew Mr. Tommy's reputation, having attended hundreds of his services over the years. He had a gift of prophecy, and the Lord would often use him to call out those who needed the most intervention. I sat and watched person after person move forward, fall on their knees, and surrender their hearts to the Lord in repentance. They were bold, broken, and weak, but strong enough to surrender, which was way more than I had in me. After they received prayer, the breakthrough was tangible on the faces of those walking away from the altar. They were almost illuminated with freedom. I just sat and watched the process; it was mesmerizing.

In response to the cry of my heart, the Lord moved on Mr. Tommy to pray for me. At first, I was horrified. This was not how I had planned for him to see me, all bare and broken instead of grown and gussied up. I was embarrassed about what a wreck I had made of things. But when this dear friend called me out, asking me to come up for prayer, it was as if I moved without will. For the first time in a while, I didn't feel like it was because the attention was on me. I felt God honestly had something to say and wanted me to hear it.

I stood before this man, who began to speak prophetically about how God had allowed me to be on a leash. He talked about how I had drifted into areas I never thought were possible. He'd allowed my heart to wander, but He wouldn't let me go too far from Him.

However, there was a limit to that leash. Though He was still hanging on, there was a word of warning: if I continued down the path of destruction I had chosen, He would let go of the leash. He loved me enough to let me choose, but at this moment, He was fighting for me. He wanted to give me beauty for ashes and hope for the future.

During that powerful encounter, I was confronted for the first time with the reality of my eating disorder. God knew! This evangelist friend was the first to address what was probably obvious to others, and I couldn't escape or deflect attention. I stared into the face of my fear of food, of gaining weight, and of who that would make me. I had been living a lie, that I had control over what I looked like and that if I could control what I looked like, I could control how people felt about me and responded to me. People would accept me if I was perfect.

At that moment, the Holy Spirit used this remarkable man's words to pour healing waters of truth, acceptance, and peace over me. The healing wasn't complete right then, but it was a beginning. I ran back into the arms of the Father I had been seeking. I felt safe, loved, and rescued from my self-made prison of control. The Lord revealed the truth to me that permeated the emptiness in my heart and assured me that no matter what my earthly father or stepfather had done, no matter what they weren't able to provide for me in the way of tenderness or meeting the needs of my heart, my heavenly Father was more than I could ever need.

The Lord wanted to love me in the way that I was desperate to be loved. He wanted to be who I would run to. So I did: I surrendered it all, once again and for the final time, giving Him my life, my disappointments, my failures, and all control.

To be sure, I would go on to make many mistakes, many of which I'll painstakingly share in the pages to come. But this moment of surrender was pivotal. As the Lord graciously helped me face my failures, I knew in that moment that I had to make some defining decisions when I walked out of that church. I knew my friends, my habits, and my way of life had to be different. I wanted them to be different!

At the same time the knowing came, so did hope. It had been a long time since I had hoped for anything. My future was something I had determined to survive on my own effort. Ambitions for anything more than that had dissipated with the compounding disappointments. However, in this Holy

Spirit moment of refreshing, something familiar awoke. Dreams began to spring forth within me. In an instant, I had hope for a future, and as I wrapped myself up in beautiful conversation with this man of God, the Lord once again spoke.

Mr. Tommy continued to share prophetically for what seemed like hours, communicating that God had already set apart a husband made just for me. This man would be after God's own heart and would fulfill my deepest desires for a partner in life. God was going to give me the dream of a beautiful marriage despite my failures. I was overcome with the mercy of a loving Father! He even shared that meeting him would be "right around the corner," but—a word of caution—I was to wait for God's clear direction.

He warned me that I should be careful not to date someone just because they were a Christian. In fact, he felt a strong sense that there was a "wolf in sheep's clothing" who would prove a distraction from God's best if I weren't careful. I was simply to wait on the Lord and not strive to make anything happen on my own.

Of course, at that moment, I thought all this would be easy. I had no need or want for anything but God in my life as Mr. Tommy spoke, and the Holy Spirit worked within me. God had done so much in my heart; I could trust Him to bring about His promise at the right time.

I walked away a new creation in Christ. I was refreshed. I was renewed. That altar call completely changed my course in life; it was pivotal because it sent me back into the arms of the Lord for good.

REFLECTION

Performance is a relentless taskmaster. God has called us to bring our best to the tasks we set our hands to, but not to make what we do into our god. In my struggle, performance became a way of masking my weakness, fear, and feelings by controlling what others were allowed to see in me. The trouble with performance is the other edge of the sword: the constant nagging in your mind, *"What happens when I can't perform?"*

The dread of always wondering when the jig will be up makes it impossible to grow through our trials and experiences. It also makes it difficult to let ourselves be loved the way God loves us, because we don't see ourselves as lovable.

When we realize the acceptance and unconditional love available to us in the person of Jesus, there's an incredible liberation from the burden of having to perform. Jesus doesn't call us to perform. He simply calls us to come to Him.

PART TWO

THE DIRT

CHAPTER FIVE

OBEDIENCE

[Live] as obedient children [of God]; do not be conformed to the evil desires which governed you in your ignorance [before you knew the requirements and transforming power of the good news regarding salvation].

—1 Peter 1:14

S hortly after graduating high school, I began working at a local department store, where my job and friendships quickly became the focus of my daily life. Naturally, after such an incredible rededication experience, I began to share with my work friends about what the Lord was doing in me.

One particular friend, whom I had bonded with more than the others, encouraged me to join the church her family attended. As it happened, I had some previous experience with a few of their young adults before I had moved to Oregon. One was my best friend, Kristen, with whom I hadn't really reconnected with since leaving so abruptly just a few months after our Beach Bum Bash escapade.

Attending church became an easy transition; regularly having a family to participate with helped me get grounded. Over time, I found this wonderful family had a room open in their house. I had just started to look for a room to rent, as I committed to my grandparents that I would find my own place after high school. They weren't pushing me in any way, but I also felt it was high time for me to be truly out on my own. I'd already been taking care of myself for a long time. Now, if I could rent a place, I would be free and in control of my future.

I offered to rent their room, continued going to church with them, and finally was living a life that I knew would lead me closer to the things of God. I had no idea, really, about what the future would look like for me, but I was making things happen and knew I had God on my side.

As life began to gain traction with my new living situation, I committed myself to be excellent in whatever I put my hands to (and to make as much money as possible). I worked two jobs and loved the sense of independence. I enjoyed the simplicity of giving my all and seeing the reward that came as a result. I excelled and was regularly recognized by my superiors as an "up and comer." One of the jobs I worked on nights and weekends was the local Pizza Hut. In just a short time, I rose through the ranks and eventually was promoted to shift manager.

In addition, the family I was renting a room from quickly became a source of stability for me. I began to bond with them the same way I had with the family I lived with in Sequim. They had a dynamic that I was attracted to. There was a healthy marriage. There was submission to the Lord. Though their kids were gone and going their own ways, a sense of support and love for their kids was evident, despite the noticeable distance between their upbringing and their lifestyle choices. The family was not perfect, but their dynamic was healthy and rooted in unconditional love.

It wasn't long before I opened my heart in a way I hadn't in a long time and allowed these people to speak into my life. I began to call them Mom and Dad. I asked them for guidance. I asked them for the kinds of boundaries kids need but often fight against. I was technically an adult, but I craved the safety of accountability.

With a newly inspired view of my future, and the security of a family environment giving me confidence, I decided to get involved with the Miss Grays Harbor program for a second time. Miss Grays Harbor was the local version of the Miss America program. I ran as a contestant at the end of my senior year of high school, and while I had great success— placing as the second runner-up—I still had a dream to go further. This time around was different, however. I had matured emotionally as I drew closer to the Lord, and this family I had come to love so dearly was giving me confidence that wasn't contingent upon proving my worth.

My experience with them also inspired a platform I was passionate about promoting: "Commitment to the American Family." I had experienced the safety and love of a family committed to one another through thick and thin. They chose a relationship with one another before ambitions, offenses, or misguided advice from supposed friends. I loved sharing my heart openly with people inspired by the message; this break from hiding was liberating. Although the nature of the program highlighted my competitiveness, I was also willing to hold this dream with an open hand.

During my first experience as a contestant just a short eighteen months before, I had met the "wolf in sheep's clothing" my evangelist friend cautioned me about. He was introduced to me by my friend (whose parents I had moved in with), was a Christian, had a career in the military, and seemed to think I walked on water. I didn't heed the evangelist's warning and became involved with him quickly. I was convinced that he would be the best I could do, given all the wrong turns I had taken in the past.

Although my relationship with the Lord was restored, my belief in my worthiness certainly was not. I didn't see myself as a prize. Instead, I saw myself as lucky to have this family that decided that they would love me. I saw myself as fortunate that the Lord would take me back—that He would forgive me and want me to be his daughter. Forgetting entirely about the warnings, I felt lucky to have a Christian man willing to overlook my shortcomings and make me his.

It didn't take long into the relationship for me to sense an unhealthy codependence forming. I didn't know what that was at the time, but I knew he was crazy about me, to the point that I feared what he would do if I ever decided I didn't want to make our relationship permanent. I didn't reciprocate his affection but simply felt that I should be grateful he liked me. I tried to find a way to appreciate that I could have a future in spite of my past.

Thankfully, the Lord intervened in His great mercy, and before I knew it, he was restationed to Phoenix, Arizona. Something within me leaped with excitement when he got restationed. Maybe I would have the opportunity to break away?

Unfortunately, he decided to propose the night before his departure, even though I had sensed his desperation and begged him not to. He figured he had enough of a hold on me that I would not be able to say no—and he was right. The next day, he moved to Phoenix, and I wore a ring I was sick to my stomach about.

A few months passed, and before I knew it, he asked me to come pay him a visit. I agreed and planned my first airplane ride a few weeks later. Still living with my "adopted" parents, I needed to borrow their credit card to complete my booking for the flight. As I mentioned earlier, one of the most beautiful dynamics with this couple was my desire to be under their authority and submit to the boundaries they thought appropriate for me. Unfortunately, when they had prayed about my taking this trip and felt strongly that I was not to go, rebellion rose in me. I determined to find a way to get there without their help.

This was a sheer act of defiance, since I didn't even want to go. But I wasn't going to let anybody tell me what I could or could not do. Nobody had really cared to do that before in my life, at least not in a way that was unselfishly for my protection. So I got a credit card from someone else, booked my ticket, and went to Phoenix.

When I landed, I immediately had the same sinking feeling I'd previously experienced when he was close. I felt completely out of control and knew it wasn't healthy. Right away, I knew I should have returned to that airport, called home, and apologized for my defiance. The sinking feeling grew into fear the second I found out the hotel he was supposed to secure for me somehow, supposedly, fell through at the last minute. I would have to stay in his barracks on the sofa with him and his roommate. Talk about the opposite of the protection my family was trying to offer!

Then the unthinkable happened: during my stay there, Brian took advantage of me in a way that I couldn't reverse, and it broke me. Here I was, having recommitted my life to the Lord and wanting to live a life of purity until I was married. And in a decision I didn't get to make but felt overwhelmingly responsible for, that commitment was broken. Why couldn't I have listened? Not only did I not heed the warning of the evangelist when I knew in my heart this was not my destiny, but I also turned my back on the loving instruction of a family I knew had zero self-interest in preventing my trip.

Shame moved in, and hiding my heart became a requirement for survival. I returned home in a silent heap of confusion, bitterness, and self-hatred. I didn't have the strength or courage to break off our engagement while I was there. I waited until my plane landed safely back in Washington and then called his mom so she could relay the message. There was no way I would tell anybody what had happened. They would find out soon enough that there wouldn't be any wedding.

When I got home, I lied about my trip, telling my family that things went fine. Then, I furiously began to pour myself into my work in a desperate attempt to distract my thoughts with so much busyness that I didn't have time for my feelings. I started a new job at a resort travel agency about thirty minutes outside town. It perfectly filled my work week, upwards of twelve hours a day. By the time I worked overtime, commuted, and grabbed a couple hours of sleep at one of the resorts we serviced, including on the weekends, I was barely home. Suddenly, I didn't have time for church, nor did I even want to converse with God. I was humiliated to face Him with my failure.

Weeks passed, and I would come home after everyone was in bed and leave before everyone got up. In my mind, though I loved God and this family He had given me, my shame had gotten the better of me. During that time, I began trying to cover my pain with anything that gave me a sense of control, eventually reintroducing all the things God had so graciously removed from me that wonderful night when He healed and renewed my heart. I knew that leash the evangelist prophesied about had been removed, and I was on my own, lost forever.

I didn't have the first clue how to continue to hide this ugly truth from my adopted family, either. I was convinced that if they knew the truth of what happened in Phoenix, and the subsequent tornado of bad choices I had made since, they would want nothing to do with me. In my mind, they would love hearing that they were right all along and would find justice in reminding me that I shouldn't have disobeyed them. I'd got what I deserved.

As the weeks turned into months, my intentional hiding was evident to my family. One Sunday afternoon, my adopted dad showed up while I was working at the resort. I looked like a deer in headlights when he walked up to the counter to say hello. I couldn't run, and I couldn't hide. I knew he could see the horror of sin all over me and must have been disgusted by what he saw looking into my eyes. What on earth was he thinking, driving forty minutes out of his way to come to my workplace? Was he going to kick me out? Had he heard rumors?

At first, I didn't think I heard him correctly when he very tenderly said that he missed me and wanted to see if I had time to grab a cup of coffee. Much to my dismay, my boss heard him come in and immediately interrupted my rejection of his offer by sending me home for the day since "things were slow." Here I was, faced with a moment I couldn't hide from. I think if he hadn't offered to drive, I would have bolted!

We went down the street to a little diner and grabbed a table in the corner. I was rude, curt, and uninterested in having any type of real conversation. He asked how I was doing, genuinely wanting to know what had been going on in my life and showing concern that I had abandoned my regular church attendance.

As he asked open-ended questions and tried to get more than one-word answers, I decided it was time to put him out of his misery. I was going to unload and tell him everything, and I mean *everything*. I was going to give him all the justification he needed to reject me for good reason. I was going to let him tell me how stupid I was and how deserving I was of everything I got, and would let him unleash the disappointment he'd no doubt have in his heart when he learned the truth of who I really was. It was time I faced the consequences and got this charade over with.

My confession felt like an out-of-body experience, as I laid my heart bare before him. I didn't want to leave out any gruesome detail so he could see fully who he was dealing with. Every hidden detail was revealed in a way I had never shared with any human. In fact, I never even confessed my sin like that to God before. The Lord already knew, of course, so I had been able to spare myself the pain of hearing the truth of what was in me from my own ears. I was numb with fear, certain of what his response would be, but I continued nonetheless. I avoided eye contact at all costs.

I told him everything that happened in Phoenix. I told him about the evangelist's warning and about the "leash." I explained how I had returned to hiding, avoiding, controlling, and covering up my pain with anything I could find to anesthetize it. I told him I had relationships that were out of control, and I engaged in anything but edifying activity. I shared the extent of my unworthiness and said I wanted to self-destruct.

I went on and on before I finally looked up. When I did, I was shocked at what I saw. While my "there you have it" attitude added sharpness to every word that came out of my mouth, what he heard brought him to tears. At that point in my life, I don't think I had ever seen a grown man cry. In fact, I was convinced that men didn't really feel emotions deeply. Now I stopped, realizing how broken he was. He had lost control of his emotions sitting in front of me, unashamedly, and in public at that.

For a moment, we just stared at each other. I was waiting for the shoe to drop and felt guilt gnawing at my gut as I realized I must have really hurt him. I was leaving him no choice but to reject me. I had no idea how painful that would be to watch, but I clearly was way too committed now.

He broke the silence when he said, "I am so sorry." Shocked and confused, I braced for the punchline, but it didn't come. He repeated it as if knowing I hadn't fully processed what he said. There was devastation in his eyes, in a way I was familiar with. I didn't understand what was going through his mind.

Suddenly, I wished I could have taken it all back. I didn't want to hurt this man who had opened his heart to me as a father when he didn't have to. What in the world would he have to be sorry for? He had never been anything but good to me, opening his home to me and trying to guide me in a way I had asked him to—and this was how I repaid him? I just sat back and stared. I was speechless, not having the slightest idea how to respond or how to move forward from here. He then broke the silence again and said, "I'm so sorry you have had to go through that all alone. If I had known, I would have loved to support you and be there for you."

I just continued to stare at him, confused at his response. And what he said next has never left me: "Trina, I don't think you realize that I love you as if you were my own. That I don't remember that I didn't bring you home from the hospital as a little baby, that you didn't come from me. You're not naturally mine, but I love you as my own. And when you hurt, I am hurting. I don't want to see you hurt, and my goal is to protect you and truly just to love you and help you become who God wants you to become."

His words were like the words of my Father God. They reached deep into my heart and spoke over me how deeply he loved me, and that my actions didn't determine whether or how much he loved me.

And I, too, broke and wept. All of the years of hiding and feeling rejected, and the insatiable need to perform, began to fall off of me at that moment. I found myself not wanting to do anything but rest in the comfort of this earthly father and find refuge in my heavenly Father. I opened my heart and allowed the Lord to heal the wound in me that had been created from that relationship I was never meant to be in.

REFLECTION

It is fascinating to me that Jesus spat in the dirt and made mud to put on the blind man's eyes. In my interpretation of the story, the spit was offensive enough, but to mix it with dirt? When we need help, we are challenged to see where our help will come from, because our view gets tainted by our circumstances. Where I see spit as offensive, saliva was considered a healing agent in the culture in which the story was written.

Also, where I see dirt as something I walk on and that I certainly don't want in my eyes, I wonder what Jesus was thinking about the dirt. Perspective changes our heart when we open it to someone we can trust to challenge our paradigms. Dirt is what we were made from, when God so lovingly breathed life into His finest creation, that which He made in His own image: *us!* The thought that Jesus might have been looking at the dirt with fondness and reflecting on the Father's original intent for man changed my perspective about the dirt.

The story, though, doesn't stop with mud in the eyes, nor did the mud instantly heal the blind man. There was a process of obedience to which the man would have to submit in order to receive the healing that was his for the taking.

Jesus asked him, with mud caked on his eyes, to wash in the Pool of Siloam. We already know from the story that the man was at the temple gate. The story doesn't talk about the distance from the gate to the pool, the steep uneven staircase, or the crowds of people he would have to navigate, in a state of blindness, to get there.

Obedience is a key to gaining freedom from our offenses. Not that it's always easy to obey or that the circumstances will be perfect, but oftentimes it's just a matter of putting one foot in front of the other and moving forward.

CHAPTER SIX

LOVED AND WANTED

Just as [in His love] He chose us in Christ [actually selected us for Himself as His own] before the foundation of the world, so that we would be holy [that is, consecrated, set apart for Him, purpose-driven] and blameless in His sight. In love [5] He predestined and lovingly planned for us to be adopted to Himself as [His own] children through Jesus Christ, in accordance with the kind intention and good pleasure of His will— [6] to the praise of His glorious grace and favor, which He so freely bestowed on us in the Beloved [His Son, Jesus Christ].

—Ephesians 1:4–6

Over the next few months, I didn't leave home much at all. I pared down my work significantly and didn't do much of anything besides go to church. I didn't want to be anywhere but near the family who had given me the safety only unconditional love could provide.

One afternoon, we were watching TV as a family, in our glorious state of "boring," when my adopted dad doubled down on the lesson of what unconditional really meant.

We were watching Home Improvement, and as in every episode, the character Tim did something stupid that hurt his wife. Tim then groveled in confusion while the audience roared in laughter. I looked up at my family in disgust and, with resolve, declared that I would never get married. I went further, claiming that I didn't want anything to do with men anymore, period. In fact, I boldly stated that if God ever wanted me to get married, He was going to have to hit me over the head with a baseball bat.

What was meant to be a light moment, an offhand remark about my vow to remain single, quickly became a sacred moment. It was one of those times when God stepped in and pinpointed the shame trying to stunt the work of healing taking place in my heart.

This appointed dad of mine immediately had the wisdom to turn off the TV and hold an intervention. For a while, he looked at me as if he were struggling to find the right word. Finally, he broke his silence and said, "I want you to know something. You are a prize, and *you* are worth fighting for!"

Then he tried to lighten things up a bit when he jokingly added, "Besides, what about that Kenny Miller guy you were so enamored with for years?" I honestly don't have a clue how he knew about that drummer at the Beach Bum Bash who had worked at the drive-in. "What if that ideal man of yours suddenly came along and swept you off your feet?"

I broke down and started to sob. What began with a funny TV show had become a moment of truth. I knew that I wasn't worthy of a man like Kenny. He was a man of God who deserved someone who had been good to the core like he was. It made my heart grieve to think how unworthy I had become in all my searching for significance.

I looked up at my dad, still unable to control my emotions, and said, "Someone like him deserves so much more than me."

Before I could even sense their sorrowful reaction to my statement, this couple, who had become an incredible example of love and acceptance to me, swallowed me up in their arms and began to pray. They ministered and spoke life into my broken heart.

After what felt like hours of hiding my shame by burying my face in my hands, I will never forget what I saw when I looked up. I locked onto the fierce gaze of this man who had become a true father to me. What I saw wasn't anger; it was the look of a defender. He stared me down and spoke with words so intensely that they still ring in my ears today.

He said, "If someone like that is the man that God has set apart for you, none of what you've done up to this point would matter, and I want you to remember that." As his words, and waves of healing truth, washed over me, I continued to cry and find comfort in their loving arms.

The truth that their unconditional love revealed was that I didn't have to perform to earn it—and that truth was transformational. I had a new hope developing in my spirit because of these two people who had so much wisdom beyond mine. The reality that they truly were guiding me from a place of love and encouragement, with a heart to help me become who I was purposed to be—and not who I thought I deserved to become or who my experiences told me I should become—propelled me toward the arms of God and to a place of true surrender.

As life continued and another year passed, it was time for the Miss Grays Harbor pageant again. On my trek for Miss America, I was now changed from the inside. I was coming from a place of sharing what was inside me with the world, on a mission to live out my dream. I wasn't hiding behind the façade of acceptance or approval. Instead, I had a message to share, and this was the way I knew how. I had been working hard all season: working out, training, developing my platform, interviewing, and sharing my heart transparently in ways I never had before. I was confident, I was content, and I was ready. I was prepared like I'd never been ready for anything else. This was going to be my time to step into destiny.

In the final weeks of preparation, we spent a lot of time in the community at local events to build awareness and practice being comfortable on a stage. One afternoon, I ran into Denna, the old friend of mine who had also worked at the drive-in before I had left for Portland. She had gotten married when I had been gone and invited me over to her place, where she lived with her husband's family.

While we sat and caught up on all the events of years past, the craziest thing happened: Kenny Miller walked into the room. I had no real idea who he was or where he lived, or for all I knew at the time, if he had gotten married himself in the years I was gone. Come to find out, Kenny was my friend's new brother-in-law. It was a fun fact, but I didn't pay too much attention at that moment. After all, I was on a mission, and he wasn't part of it.

Now, I falsely assumed that my crush on this man all this time wasn't known by anyone but my friend Kristen, who must have forgotten by now. Much to my surprise, it was widely known—seemingly by everyone. Once Denna realized I would be in the pageant, she planned to bring her husband and cheer me on. At some point, she wound up mentioning it to her brother-in-law, who incidentally had also decided that he wanted to come to watch.

I didn't know any of that at the time, so when he called me at the office and said, "This Ken Miller," I literally fell off my chair. He asked how he could get tickets to the event. I answered his questions and awkwardly got off the phone as quickly as I could. After I hung up, I sat dumbfounded. I couldn't deny the little spark I felt in my heart, even though I quickly pushed it aside.

Unbeknownst to me, my dad had been talking to Kenny, learning who he was and what he was all about. He didn't tell me until much later, but he realized that Kenny had been praying for his wife for years. Although he'd been hounded endlessly by family and friends about finding a mate, he had committed to the Lord that he was only going to date the girl he would marry and was content to wait until she was revealed to him. He wasn't going to waste his time or share his heart; he was going to save himself and his emotions by waiting on the Lord.

I didn't know that Kenny had been spending extra time praying for his wife in the days leading up to this pageant event. He had been growing a bit weary of the wait but also wanted to continue being intentional about giving his desire for a wife to the Lord completely. In fact, Kenny was feeling like he wanted to pursue something with me but wanted to be sure it was God leading him before he said anything. So he decided to make a deal with God on his way to the venue that night. The deal was that if I won the title and had the chance to continue to the next level, he would move on, knowing there were other plans in store for me. If I didn't win, he would step out in faith as a response to what he thought he was sensing: a relationship God was seeding in his heart.

Just a few hours later, when I was called first runner-up and not the winner, I found that I myself still needed to relinquish some control. I was devastated and confused. I'd been working hard for this, and I knew I had performed at my best. I couldn't understand why I didn't get to have this opportunity that was such a big dream of mine. At least, I thought it was a dream.

In reality, though, the actual dream was the one I had in my heart for a man like Kenny to come and sweep me off my feet and give me a family who would chase after the Lord together. That dream was too big, in my mind. It was one I had given up on, because I had gone too far and blown any possibility of receiving God's best. I thought I was on the path to the backup plan, with a few of my chosen pit stops on the journey.

I eventually realized, through peeling back the layers the coming season would bring, that this pageant goal became a dream only after I found a need for attention. It was born from the need to prove to everyone around me that I was worthy of a title and recognition. My pageant dream was almost like one big temper tantrum.

I didn't realize what else was being orchestrated that night—and rightfully so, as I'm sure I would have gotten in the way. God didn't need my help with this one! My best friend Kristen, who had been the first to know of my affections for this young drummer, took the liberty of arranging a post-pageant dinner party. She made all the arrangements. I was the last to find out about it, as we were eating cake and collecting flowers at the reception, but I just had to show up.

W had a great time at the dinner. There were six of us laughing, playing games, and enjoying each other's company. I couldn't ignore, though, a heavy feeling in my heart. I was still so raw, wounded, and unprepared for what was (obviously) on everyone's mind—or for any kind of relationship. I didn't want anyone to have hope for something that could never be, in my mind. It was an odd place for me. I thrived off of getting what I wanted and making things happen. Yet, I was tapping the brakes to ensure nobody, especially Kenny, got the wrong idea.

As the night wrapped up, Kenny offered to walk me to the car. He grabbed all the games I had brought and tried to keep up as I bolted out the door, hoping to get in the car and be ready to pull out of the parking lot before things got weird. I could feel myself welling up as I heard him walking behind me. He popped the games in the back seat as I was buckling up, and I quickly said goodbye and shut the door in his face.

As I drove away, I felt like a moron, but I also found myself completely terrified. I knew of his relationship commitment by this point, and I was horrified that he would even entertain the likes of me. All I could think was how embarrassing it would be to tell him that I had a "scarlet letter" I couldn't shake. I'd have to tell him I wasn't who I seemed to be or who I let people see on a stage. I was a fraud, and he deserved better.

I didn't have time to entertain precisely how I would have the conversation I just described. Hence, I decided I would just put off the "not interested" vibe. Since Kenny didn't know what was happening inside me, forward steps toward a relationship seemed to be gearing up. Dinner events, group activities, and several opportunities to be together piled on, over the following weeks. I found myself at events packed with his family and friends, who were clearly excited that Kenny might be interested in someone.

If they only knew! The pressure started getting to me, since I had no intention of actually carrying on this charade. Even though Kenny and I didn't interact a lot one on one, I could tell that his affections were growing. I couldn't bear it. I did not want to give him hope and then dash his dreams once he found out who I really was. It wouldn't be fair to put him in a position of having to reject me because I didn't line up with his expectations.

I worked myself into a complete state of turmoil. I couldn't sleep. I tried avoiding all my sappy friends who smiled incessantly and planned ridiculous parties. All these wonderful people were hoping, even expecting, a reality that would never be. I didn't want to be the cause of hurting any of them.

One morning, following yet another dinner party at Kenny's brother's house, I got a call from Kristen. She had no idea what a mess I had become about this entire business. Rather, she assumed I was living in some surreal experience of a Cinderella story with my childhood crush. She greeted me with her distinctive sing-songy voice, which at that moment was like nails on a chalkboard to my tormented soul. She asked me how my evening went, even though I knew she didn't care but must have something to tell me. I barely got the word "fine" out of my mouth when she said she had just received the cutest phone call from Kenny: he was wondering if she could help him figure out what to buy me for Christmas.

What? This was clearly going too far. I stopped her in her tracks and told her how distraught I had been and how I hadn't been sleeping, agonizing instead about how this would come to an end. I told her that I was not who he'd been waiting for, that I didn't want to hurt him, and that I didn't want to get hurt. I told her the second that he found out about my past, everything would just blow up and get ugly—so he really shouldn't get me anything for Christmas!

She didn't seem phased at all by my admission. In fact, she kind of giggled a bit. Then she said, "It's funny, last night, he told me he had also been up all night, talking with his brother. He told his brother that he knows you're his wife."

I broke down completely at her words and said, "No, I'm not! He thinks I am something I can't live up to, and he doesn't know anything about my past. He would be devastated if he knew the real me. I can't disappoint him that way."

Kristen was quiet for a minute after my rant before saying, "It's interesting you bring that up. He actually knows all about your past." I was shocked and a little horrified. First, I had no idea how he would have known, but I also didn't care because the truth was revealed. I didn't have to endure the pain of breaking the bad news.

She didn't know who his source of information was, but the next words that came out of her mouth broke the very chain that had been holding me back. Kristen said, "He knows that God has set you apart for him; none of what you've done up to this point matters." That was exactly what my adopted dad had said to me just a few months earlier.

It was time to let go and let God move. The walls came down when I heard those words, but with trepidation. I was at least willing to see what God was up to, instead of being so guarded.

REFLECTION

Unconditional love was a concept I couldn't comprehend, even with the understanding that Jesus sacrificed His life to rescue me from my sin. I had become so steeped in my ability to prove my worth and make people love me, the reality of Christ loving me even when I chose to sin escaped my comprehension. When He revealed His love for me by seeing my secret desire to belong to a family who loved me despite my shortcomings, and to have a husband who had been set apart for the moment God would reveal whom He had chosen for him, it overwhelmed me. That kind of vulnerability helped me discover what living under the shadow of His wing (read Psalm 91!) was all about.

When we take refuge in God, we find strength in His peace and protection. Truth can be heard because we are safe in a secret place. God's love is beyond our comprehension. There's not a single person I know who would allow their child to be sacrificed for another, let alone for someone who doesn't even grasp what's being offered. The only way we can take hold of the truth of God's deep, wide, unconditional love for us is to find refuge in Him. We must let Him fully envelop our hearts and minds. Even then, we only get a glimpse of His love—but I'm here to tell you that it's liberating!

CHAPTER SEVEN

The Desire of My Heart

Delight yourself in the LORD,
And He will give you the desires and petitions of your
heart.
⁵ Commit your way to the LORD;
Trust in Him also and He will do it.

—**Psalm 37:4–5**

T he holiday season flew by, and before I knew it, Christmas was just two days away. Like many evenings over the last several weeks, Kenny and his family invited me to dinner. What I didn't know was that it was their family Christmas celebration.

After a beautiful dinner, I sat and awkwardly watched them open all their gifts for each other. At the end of the pile was a letter for me. It turned out to be a scavenger hunt. As embarrassing as it was for me to have his family watch me go through their entire house to find this gift, my heart was in disbelief that this could be happening. With a small gesture (which turned out to be a giant teddy bear), I knew in my heart what was developing. I marveled, *"God, could You really be doing this for me?"*

Up to this point, while we had spent a lot of time with family and friends, Kenny and I had never had a private conversation or a one-on-one date. One evening shortly after Christmas, I was feeling the need to get out and get some exercise. It would be a great way to process all my emotions and empty my mind a bit of the whirlwind of the previous couple weeks. Kenny wasn't feeling great about me being outside by myself after dark, so he insisted on coming with me.

He picked me up at home and drove me to our local middle school track. Naturally, I was kind of nervous. What were we going to talk about, just the two of us? I wasn't sure I was ready for the pressure of the next step.

As we started walking, he immediately started sharing about the commitment he had made with God to wait on a relationship until he knew God was leading him. God was intentionally the center of his world, and he trusted the Lord to put the right person in his life. He didn't want to waste his time or sacrifice any piece of his heart, or hurt anyone else in the process. He was committed to purity and knew that wasn't a common practice, even in the church world. I already admired his resolve but was even more drawn to him when I heard the conviction in his heart to remain faithful to his promise, no matter how difficult it was or how weird others thought he was.

There was no going back after hearing the next couple of words that came out of his mouth. They weren't so eloquently, but they were as sweet and pure as imaginable: "So, do you want to be my girlfriend?"

I didn't even know how to respond. While I remained quiet and stammering a bit, there was no denying the spark in my heart that I knew God was up to something amazing. I didn't give him any kind of a straight answer right away. In fact, I kept avoiding the question.

We got in the car after a few more laps, and as he prepared to drive me home, he said, "You never answered my question."

I opened my heart a smidge and let him see a glimpse of my fear when I replied, "I feel like there's just no going back, and I want to be careful that it's right for you."

He immediately put me at ease, eager to hear if I was experiencing the same feelings as he was. I eventually gave an unenthusiastic, "Well, I suppose," answer. While it wasn't the resounding *yes* he was hoping to hear, I knew he understood my trepidation.

When we got to my house, and he dropped me off at the door, I went inside awkwardly, not knowing exactly where we were to go from there. As the door was closing, I heard for the first time words I would cherish for a lifetime. He said, "I love you, girl," and as he said it, the door shut coldly in his face before I had a chance to respond.

I stood behind the closed door, frozen in time. It was a clash of the overwhelming reality that my heart's desire was right there in front of me, sheer terror, and a ton of embarrassment. His first profession of feelings for a woman, after all the years of waiting, ended up with a door shut in his face. I didn't know what to do. Should I open the door and acknowledge that I heard him, or was it better to leave the door closed and pretend like I didn't hear him?

Unfortunately, I chose the safe path and left him there, hoping he would think I didn't hear him. I tried to just go to bed and put my mind at rest, but sleep wouldn't come. I was elated. I had admired him for so long, and I still couldn't believe that he would be interested in someone like me.

The next step was to start going to church together; it was the Christian way of putting our status on Facebook, I guess. We also created the habit of spending dedicated prayer time together. Foundationally, we wanted to put God first. I don't think either of us realized how critical that decision would be in our future years, when we would face the fight of our lives. At the moment, though, when we cranked up worship music in the giant auditorium of the church, just the two of us, pacing the floors and singing with all our hearts to celebrate the goodness of God, it truly couldn't have been any better. It felt like we were floating a bit.

With the start of a new year, there came a season of prayer and preparation in our church body to seek God for what was to come. Our church would come together nightly for seven days and simply pray. While Ken and I were moving forward relationally, I still had a lingering fear in my heart that he couldn't fully understand the extent of my lifestyle choices, or else he wouldn't have chosen to pursue me. I knew at some point that I would have to sit down and tell him everything. I dreaded the thought.

On the way to prayer one evening, my nightmare became a reality when he said, "I know that you have a past, and you have a lot that you've walked through in life that I haven't experienced. We've never really talked about that, but I'd like to talk about it."

The bomb had been dropped. I knew these weeks of hope, anticipation, and bliss couldn't be my reality. I only had one choice: to bring it to God in prayer. Since we were already on our way, I certainly would have the opportunity. I was immediately assuming this experience would be coming to an end. I felt so foolish for letting my guard down.

Just earlier that same day, I talked to my friend Kristen while on my way to work. I told her I couldn't get June 17 out of my mind. She laughed and said, "That's because it's the day you're going to get married. I'm going to put it on my calendar right now!"

Horrified, I begged her not to write it anywhere and made her promise that she wouldn't repeat that statement to anyone. Our long-ago moment, giggling about Kenny and me like the schoolgirls we were back then, was now haunting me. I was reminded how stupid it was to have let this relationship develop. I knew better.

I barely remember walking into the church that night. I mainly recall how unbearable it felt to be begging the Lord to help me remember every painful detail of my past. If we were going to have this talk, we would only do it once. I wanted it *all* out there, without misrepresenting myself in any way. My attitude was dramatically different from the defensive posture I had taken with my adopted dad six months before. I was now in a place of complete surrender. At the very least, Kenny deserved full transparency, and if God was orchestrating all of this, I needed to trust them both—completely.

By the end of prayer, I was ready. God had so lovingly reminded me that He was all I needed, and if Ken made a different choice due to my confession, God's love for me was still the same. Courage filled my bones in a way I had never experienced. Now I just needed to figure out how to start the conversation.

After prayer, we drove to the Hoquiam airport and parked the car. There was a silence, but a peaceful one, as Kenny spoke. I felt like he must have read my mind when he said, "I'm sure you don't know how to begin, but I just want to ask you questions. There are some things I'm curious about."

As he asked, I was overcome with shame. I didn't let that derail me from answering honestly, though. No matter how difficult it was, I didn't want to leave any detail untold. I couldn't make eye contact with him, but I didn't hold back, either.

When I stopped, I briefly looked over at him and saw that he was crying. I had to fight the urge to run at that point. I had hurt him deeply. He deserved the best God had to offer, yet somehow, he had gotten mixed up with me. I would be responsible for him breaking his commitment to the Lord all these years.

We sat in silence again. After a few minutes, he looked up at me, and said, "I am so sorry. I'm just so sorry that you've been through all of that in your life." He continued, "I know that was not the plan God had for you, but I'm so glad He has forgiven you and restored you."

That was it? Here I was, just like with my adopted dad, sitting in awe of his acceptance of me. I still thought our relationship was over, but at least I wasn't condemned. I was walking in a place of restoration. If this was simply an exercise in putting trust in God and finding our courage in Him, it was worth it.

Kenny wasn't done talking, though. Next, he wanted to address what only God could have put on his heart, which was my anorexia. I was so ashamed of it but didn't recognize that it was a chain of control still binding me. I was terrified of being overweight and being unattractive. My looks were how I got people to notice and like me. How could I live without that?

He said, "I want you to know that when we grow old together, if you ever get to be overweight, I will still love you. You're going to be my wife forever."

Wait—*what?* Grow old? Wife? He was not going anywhere, apparently. God was not just bringing me to a place of restoration. He was bringing me to a place of redemption. I could physically feel the shame coming off of me. I saw a future and a hope, and it was all sitting in front of me despite my colossal failures. On top of that, God led Kenny to see a part of my heart that He wanted to heal. The Lord was giving him the wisdom to understand what I needed for me to be able to relax and release myself—to be loved.

A couple of months later, since we knew marriage was inevitable, we started to talk about when. As it turned out, the only weekend we could find that worked within all the events of the year happened to be June 17. God does have a sense of humor, doesn't He? We had three months to plan, but the day couldn't come fast enough.

Our wedding gift from Kenny's mom and dad was a beautiful piece of property right next to them, almost an acre. We decided to build a home on it. The setting couldn't have been more ideal. On the other side of his parents were his brother and my friend Denna, with their little girls. Plus, we could have my sister's kids around. Our quiver was full with our nieces to play with and this great life we were putting together.

I certainly didn't want to mess with perfection. The place in my heart that dreamt of being a mom was content just to be an auntie. The thought of having my own kids, who might experience what I had seen in life, was overwhelming. Besides, I was terrified of being responsible for someone else's life. The decision was made: we weren't going to have children.

God had different plans, though. About four years of married life went by when we decided we wanted to start a family. We began trying to get pregnant, but I couldn't shake this nagging in the back of my mind that my anorexia had caused some fertility issues. We hadn't really told anyone we were trying, nor had I uttered a word to Kenny about my fears of being unable to conceive.

One afternoon, I attended a ladies' event at the church. The guest speaker was powerful and had some time to pray individually for women at the end of the event. She had quite a reputation for praying specifically for women in the area of fertility. At first, there was no way on God's green earth I would go up and ask her to pray for me to get pregnant, but after some coaxing, I decided that having her pray over me, in general, would be a blessing.

I'm pretty sure I was the last person in the room, but I nonetheless took the opportunity to ask. She started out praying a lovely but typical prayer, probably one she might pray over any ladies she didn't know. Then, she stopped suddenly, like she was being interrupted. She was silent for a while before finally saying, "Yeah, Lord, I hear you. Okay."

Immediately, she removed her hands from my shoulders and put them on my tummy. With more authority than I have ever heard in prayer, she started commanding my womb to conceive in the name of Jesus. The Lord had spoken to her heart that there was a baby already in there, though it had not implanted yet. After she finished praying, she told me to buy a bassinette and set it up in my room. I was to pray over that baby and thank God for putting him in my womb every day.

I did everything as she said and fell in love before I knew who I was carrying. Since this was our first child, Kenny and I decided we were not going to find out the gender until the day our baby was born. God had put clarity in my heart, however; I knew I would have a son and his name would be Josiah. My husband didn't like that name so much, but during my pregnancy, I often asked him to read me the story of King Josiah, until he got used to saying the name. We only bought boy things and only had a boy's name picked out.

At my baby shower, a good friend of ours, Mike, felt a strong calling to pray and prophesy over the baby in my womb. He spoke of the child's anointing with people and how he would love music and find his life's calling through ministry.

In July, when Josiah was born, we learned his name meant, "Jehovah has healed," and that was it. We were at a loss, undone, amazed, enamored, and in awe of the gift God gave us in Josiah. Never in a million years did I think I could love anybody as much as I loved this baby.

We had so much fulfillment being parents that a couple of years later, it seemed natural to try again. Pregnancy came easy this time, and we were awestruck that God would entrust us with another baby to love and call our own. This time we had a beautiful little girl, Trinity. She was just as fun to have around as her brother, and she brought joy with her sweet, pure disposition, just like her daddy.

Life really couldn't have been more ideal. I had a career in a field I loved with an opportunity for growth. We had two amazing kids, Kenny had a successful business, and God was the center of it all.

The most difficult thing was leaving those precious babies to go to work every day. Fortunately, my sister had an in-home daycare and loved having her niece and nephew as part of her daily routine. However, I struggled with the tug-of-war in my heart. I wanted to be with them every second but also loved having a career. The balance was challenging, and I longed for more hours in the day, more flexibility in my work, and more time to nurture my real passion—those kids!

I couldn't fathom the thought of adding any more to our crew. Plus, we had a boy and a girl. What more could we want? We thought it prudent to have Kenny visit the doctor and make sure we would stay complete as a family of four, permanently.

REFLECTION

I love to read stories where you can see full circle the redemptive heart of God. Twenty-seven years later, I still feel like I should pinch myself when I reflect on what God was giving me in that season of life. He was fully redeeming a lonely childhood and fulfilling the desires of my heart in a way that I still find miraculous.

When we get a glimpse of how God weaves our history, choices, and submission with the future He has for us, we cannot help but stay in awe of His goodness. Redemption is in His nature; we've seen it from the beginning of time, over and over again.

One of my favorite books in the Bible is the book of Ruth. Naomi's story in that book is about how God redeems even the worst of circumstances and creates beauty from ashes. The great news for us today is that His nature hasn't changed.

He delights in fulfilling our deepest desire and has a plan for each of us far beyond what we could ever ask or imagine.

CHAPTER EIGHT

THE FAITH OF A CHILD

But first and most importantly seek (aim at, strive after) His kingdom and His righteousness [His way of doing and being right—the attitude and character of God], and all these things will be given to you also.

—Matthew 6:33

There were many things we tried to be intentional about while surviving the craziness of having a young family with two working parents. That included having them in church, serving in some capacity, and making sure they understood how much God desired to be the center of every part of their lives, even the mundane.

Our devotions were called Doughnut Time. The doughnuts were simply a practical way to keep their attention for a few minutes so we could dive into biblical principles, teach them about prayer, and associate family time with something to look forward to. We wanted our kids to know that God wanted a relationship with them, loved them more they could imagine, and would always be with them.

One night as I was tucking Josiah into bed, he told me he wanted a little brother. I chuckled, knowing that would be impossible, but I didn't want to dismiss what I could see as one of those tender moments where he revealed part of his heart. All I could do with that was push him toward prayer. So I smiled and told him that request would have to be something he took to Jesus.

We then prayed, as we always did, with him going first. I found so much delight in hearing his little voice talk to God the way he did his friends, us, and anyone else he knew loved and adored him. There was such an innocence and freedom in his words, a freedom that was an outward expression of a deep trust, knowing that he was heard. He prayed sincerely and simply, asking Jesus for a little brother (as he would for many nights to come) and for a drink with the "star on the can" (he had gotten a few sips of my Rockstar a time or two, but I would never let him have it).

Like any good parent who wants their kids to know that God answers prayer, I decided to sneak an almost empty can of Rockstar onto his nightstand. Maybe that would distract him from the fact that the other request was never going to happen.

Life with these little kids seemed to fly by like an uncontrollable freight train. It was impossible to slow down, and we were desperately looking for ways to pause as often as possible to just take it all in.

One of those uncontrollable days came the day Trinity started kindergarten. Our little girl couldn't possibly be old enough to go to school! Kenny and I went with her to drop her off, meet the class, and assure her we would be there to pick her up at the end of the day. It was a big deal to think of leaving her there and knowing what an enormous milestone it was for us as a family.

We were escorted into the cafeteria with the other kids, some of whom had been dropped off while most others were accompanied by just one parent to send them off. We must have been a sight with our faces of dread, mourning the day that had come too soon. I'm sure those other parents thought we were crazy, as most giddily shooed their kids off, encouraging their independence.

The teacher had us all gather around while she read a story to the kids about leaving home for the first time to go to school. She wasn't two pages into the book when the tears (not Trinity's) started to flow. I don't know where they all came from, but I'm pretty sure it was all the way from my toes. Embarrassed at my inability to slow them down, I looked over at Kenny for some support and comfort, only to find that he, too, was overcome. We were quite a sight.

Trinity was entirely okay and one hundred percent ready for us to leave. In fact, I don't even think she said goodbye (she was probably embarrassed) as her dad and I walked toward the door. Kenny and I, on the other hand, still hadn't gotten our emotions under control. We walked silently to our separate cars, trying to gather ourselves enough to go to work. We simply waved at each other and didn't speak, to avoid a full-on meltdown.

When we got home that evening, the recognition of where we were in our life stage was all too real. The kids were getting older, and it was all going way too fast. I had prayed for years that I would be able to be home with the kids, as I felt like I was missing way too much being away all day. I wanted to enjoy the experience of being with my babies. At the same time they were young, unfortunately, I found myself working fifty miles from home. I was more distant, while my kids were taking steps toward independence. Needless to say, I was not ready and desperately wanted to get off this speed train.

I wound up getting an offer to work from home, which was exactly what would allow me to participate in the daily events of the kids while working. It was a recruiting/sales opportunity where I would get paid for directly placing people in jobs for a well-known big-box retailer. It was risky because it was only commission pay. Still, the opportunity to be able to work at home was a clear answer to prayer, so I jumped at it. I enjoyed getting to pick up my kids from school and be with them in the afternoons.

As the routine settled in and my heart began to relax, the dreamer in me again awoke. Since I was home all day long, I began to imagine what it would be like if we could have another baby. I had heard of people who had vasectomy reversals but thought it was unattainable for us. It had already been about five years at this point, so I wasn't really sure if we would be candidates for it or not.

I secretly looked online a bit, just to see how much something like that would cost. The surgery had about an $8,500 price tag and was definitely not covered by insurance. I eventually mentioned it to Kenny, who laughed it off lightly, as if to say, "You're dreaming." I was going to have to lay that dream down since there was no way we would be able to pull it off. But the seed of hope had been planted, nonetheless.

One afternoon a couple of months later, my mom came to see the kids for a day visit. Not having any idea about my secret wish, she told me a story of her church friend who was celebrating the birth of a new baby that was the result of vasectomy reversal. I'm sure the look on my face must have surprised her, but I quickly told myself to play it cool and not say anything. I listened as she shared about the urologist she'd found who was a Christ follower and had a heart for couples who wanted to add to their families. His heart was to donate his services if the recipient simply paid for the medical supplies and such.

I don't know why my mom felt compelled to share the story with me, but the conversation watered the seed that had already been planted. I subtly asked about the doctor and then gave him a call shortly after she left the house. He was genuine, and so was the story of his calling. What was God up to? The ancillary fees were only $1,500, and we had to get ourselves to Muskogee, Oklahoma. We made the appointment and planned the trip.

Everything happened so fast that I don't think we told many people. That time seems like such a blur, but I remember being in awe that we would even have this opportunity. Just a few weeks later, when we got to Oklahoma and were praying together before meeting the doctor, I couldn't stop the flow of tears. I was overwhelmed that we were there and we could possibly have the opportunity of another baby. Kenny went through the procedure with flying colors and was told we had at least an eighty percent chance of conceiving again. It didn't seem real! God was fulfilling my heart's desires yet again. He was showing the depth of His love in answering these prayers for my family.

Within a couple of months, we were pregnant. Unfortunately, that first pregnancy resulted in miscarriage, and doubt crept in. Even though we had seen God work miraculously, the fear of disappointment threatened to steal the dream in my heart. I needed to remind myself that I didn't force this to happen. God was in control, and our ability to add to our family was one hundred percent in His hands. I knew I had seen Him move; after all, the failed pregnancy was evidence of that. It was time to lean on His sovereignty and not on my lack of understanding.

So that's what we did: we just decided to wait on His timing. It wasn't long in the waiting before the dream became a reality. We found out in August 2008 that we were pregnant again. (Interesting fact: those dollar store pregnancy tests work. But a note of advice: don't leave a positive pregnancy test in the church trash can while attending a youth event. It causes unnecessary drama!)

The pregnancy was fairly uneventful until the end. I was on the border of high risk at age thirty-four, but not quite over that mark. In fact, everything looked great from the get-go, so we certainly didn't anticipate any issues. I went in for the last ultrasound at thirty-eight-and-a-half weeks to check his size and health before birth.

Quickly, it became one of those moments you dread, when everything gets quiet and the tech says, "I'm going to have to get the doctor." She wouldn't tell me why, and she wouldn't show me the screen. Thankfully, my sister-in-law, Denna, was with me, so she started praying and stepped out to call Kenny.

Eventually, the doctor and technician both came back in. After looking at the screen and confirming what the technician had seen, the doctor said, "Your baby's only about three pounds." How on earth could that be? He was due in a week. He continued to explain that the baby's head was tracking normal but that his body was disproportionately small, demonstrating some distress. The radiologist had already called ahead to the children's hospital about ninety miles away. He secured a spot for me to have a high-level ultrasound to see if there was a way to see, in more detail, what was happening in utero.

Unfortunately, they couldn't see the issue with the high-level ultrasound at the children's hospital, so I was admitted for a larger series of tests to be completed. I couldn't understand why they wouldn't just go ahead and take him out! I was so confused, thinking that he was thirty-nine weeks already and there was no reason why he wouldn't be better off outside if his environment was compromised.

Every test they ran produced more questions than answers. My doctor felt that the best option was to keep him in utero in hopes he would gain some weight before birth. They decided to let me go home on the condition that I would return every other day for a non-stress test and have a weekly amniocentesis to check his lung maturity. It was the longest three weeks of my life, waiting for them to finally feel comfortable enough to induce labor. By this time, I was ten days overdue.

Just a few short hours into labor, he went into distress, and the doctor decided to do a C-section. Since I already had the epidural, they were able to have me in the operating room within five minutes of the decision. As it turned out, my epidural wasn't strong enough, but there wasn't time to waste. They put me fully under while delivering Jude. He was born blue and had to be resuscitated, but praise God, he came through perfectly at 4 pounds and 15 ounces.

It wasn't an accident that it was Passover that day. We were spared tragedy and became the proud new parents of a perfectly healthy, but very small, baby boy! My fantastic doctor waited around for me in the recovery room to tell me personally after I woke up that Jude was okay. When he pulled him out, he could see that his umbilical cord was tied in a complete knot. It wasn't around his neck or anything; they would have seen that. They couldn't see the knot that had essentially put a "kink in the hose" so the nutrients were not getting through. We had indeed been passed over.

REFLECTION

When I reflect on Passover, I'm both expectant and amazed at the faith of God's people in the Old Testament. They werer expectant because they had seen God move miraculously around them and on their behalf. It must have been marvelous to feel heard by God when a deliverer came to their rescue—moreover, to see God show up to defend them by sending plagues on their oppressor. I'm amazed at their tremendous faith on that significant first Passover day.

This people-group knew God had heard their cry, and they had seen His wrath carried out over and over in their defense. But to think of the terror that must have enveloped their hearts and minds with the thought of what could happen if they weren't passed over! I don't know about you, but even after I have had promises come to me from God, it's a battle to stand on those promises when the intense reality of circumstances comes against me.

In my imagination, the Israelites must have meticulously followed Moses' instructions to a T, preparing the lamb and spreading the blood over their door posts. What must have gone through their mind, though, when they heard evidence all around them (on what I'm sure was a very long night) of the final plague—the death of the firstborn? What a terrifying and humbling experience! To be so vulnerable and reliant on a promise of deliverance, despite what is happening all around, takes great faith.

We've already seen God as Father, Friend, and Redeemer in this story. This reflection is all about Him being our Deliverer.

CHAPTER NINE

TRUST IN DARKNESS

As for God, His way is blameless and perfect; the word of the LORD is tested. He is a shield to all those who take refuge and trust in Him.

—2 Samuel 22:31

We enjoyed every minute of having Jude in our family. The older kids adored him. He charmed everyone who came across his path and brought joy to the most mundane of days. Every part of his personality inspired hope and was a reminder of the stewardship required when walking out a dream come true. I had a renewed spark in my belly and knew in my heart that we weren't done with change.

One might think a new baby after seven years would have been enough change for one season. In fact, I had regular nightmares about forgetting Jude places because it had been so long since I had thought about the practical aspects of being a new mom again. Nonetheless, there was a churning in my stomach and a sense of knowing that change was coming.

Just two months after Jude came home, I decided to take him and the older kids to visit their godparents and longtime friends of ours in Las Vegas. Thanks to my home office schedule, I could do my work from anywhere, so I planned to stay for a couple of weeks. Kenny couldn't get away from his work, so he decided to stay behind and keep his business running.

At some point on the trip, I interviewed for a job I hadn't gone looking for. The fact of the matter was that Kenny and I had always dreamed of moving to a new state to adventure with our kids while they were young. As we laughed together on the phone that night about my interviewing for a job in another state without him there, the spark of "what if?" began to fuel the fire of a new dream. Ultimately, we concluded that since Josiah was about to enter middle school, if we were going to try a move, we'd better do it now.

I accepted the job before leaving and then went home to prepare. We were packing up our life and moving to Nevada! Sometimes I reflect on this decision and am stunned at the courage God gave us to step forward into so many unknowns and so much uncertainty. Kenny had a successful construction business that he would leave behind while I went to work in an entirely commission-based job—selling timeshares, of all things. That didn't slow us down, though. Immediately, we were provided with someone to rent our house, and within just a couple of weeks, we had found a fully furnished rental in Las Vegas.

It was clear that God was on the move, and we were stepping headlong into our destiny without an ounce of fear. If there was a smidge of trepidation, it was overshadowed by an overwhelming sense of purpose and opportunity far beyond what we could ever ask or think. Many people were covering us in prayer. We had multiple confirmations that we were going through a door that was clearly being opened for us. Though we had no idea what we were about to walk through, we proceeded.

Just two months after the first conversation about this crazy adventure, we loaded our kids in the car and started driving. Before we knew it, we were there and settled in the little, furnished house we rented—and feeling like fish out of water. Here we were, so suddenly in a foreign place by ourselves. Though we had dreamed about this, the dream didn't seem as exciting as we attempted to navigate the day-to-day of life.

The simplest of tasks became big. Registering our kids for school, finding the grocery store, figuring out where to attend church, locating doctors and dentists—you name it, we had to start over. One Godsend in all this was that we had twenty-year lifelong friends just down the street from us, who had committed to helping us on the journey. I'm not sure we ever could have considered a move that far away without their support, especially we had a new baby to think about. Jude was only four months old when we made the move, and though he was doing well, leaving him with a complete stranger while we were working and the kids were at school would have been a deal breaker.

Ken had grown his construction business from scratch. He had gotten to a place where he consistently worked with a solid customer base. His willingness to lay that down and be open to embarking on a new adventure is still remarkable to me. That amazing responsiveness would continue to be demonstrated in the years to come, in exemplary ways.

Once I started my job, it wasn't long before I realized the amount of pressure I would be under in that commission-based environment. The reality that we had left the security of our home, family, business, and steady paychecks only added to the that pressure. It became almost unbearable at moments, as I struggled to succeed in my new career's early days. I felt incredibly responsible for all the risks we were taking, and it didn't appear to be working out.

Sales in a "one-call close" environment were proving to be a struggle. The lack of income from not selling, while we had three kids to care for and Ken needed time to get licensed to start up his business, took me to a place of sheer despair. The courage to dream seemed to be a colossal mistake. I was coming home at night in a puddle of tears, unable to emerge from the pit of feeling lost and desperate for something to go well. I felt like I was on the verge of breaking the thing I loved most: my family. This dream of mine had gotten the best of me, and I was in real trouble.

Fortunately, God was on the move. A deep-rooted self-dependence had taken hold of me as a little girl, and now He was working that out of me. I certainly couldn't see that at the time, but His grace and gentle direction spoke to my heart and allowed me to take baby steps toward a deeper level of trust in Him to care for my needs. In addition, He wanted to remind me that I was not on my own. He had put me in the care of my husband's capable arms. I didn't have to struggle alone.

By the grace of God, I learned how to use the gifts that He had given me. I knew how to connect with people. I was passionate about their family experiences, and they could feel it. I bonded with people on a deep level and earned the right to consult them on how to create memories that would last way beyond the frivolous. I released myself from the hold my success, or lack thereof, had on me. Instead, I now held each opportunity with an open hand and trusted that as I did the right thing, the success would simply be a byproduct. I began to serve those around me intentionally, regardless of whether they ultimately wanted me to fail or get out of the way. I wanted *them* to succeed. That paradigm shift began a tidal wave of blessing that was far beyond what I could have comprehended at the time.

Financially, I was blown away by the outcome. More significant than that, though, I developed a deep passion for the industry that brought me (literally) to my knees. I couldn't believe that someone could be so successful while having so much fun and doing something with so much lasting meaning. My instantaneous success grabbed the attention of people around me who had been willing me to give up just a few months before. It was truly remarkable to open my heart, coach the naysayers, and see them gain success, too.

The pressure relief resurrected the dream Ken and I had set out to fulfill with the adventure we were on. We began to enjoy the new place and make new friends as we committed to engage fully in the experience.

When we registered our kids for school, one of the first couples we met turned out to be pastors who had recently moved from Alabama with a dream to plant a church. They had one child in Trinity's class and one in Josiah's. We immediately bonded with them in a way that could only have been supernaturally ordained. Over time, the desire we'd had to sit in the back row of a megachurch, to finally take a break from serving, wore off. We wanted to partner with the vision of our friends to love on the people of Las Vegas. So, for the next few months, we began to immerse ourselves in the life of this small but wonderful church called Destiny.

We had found our tribe, our community. Little did we know that transition would be pivotal to our survival in the coming year. That church body, and another strategically placed family, became our lifeline of strength.

The other family were friends taking a break from ministry to park in Vegas and recover mentally from the toll church life can bring. Eric had started in the same industry as me, just a few months earlier than I did. He would often pray with his guests and do marriage counseling instead of selling. Ken and I quickly discovered that Eric and his wife, Cindy, were kindred spirits. The little community of people around us was more than we could have ever expected to find in Las Vegas, of all places. We were all transplants in similar stages of family life and personal growth, and with a common bond of loving the Lord.

REFLECTION

Stepping into the unknown is scary and exhilarating all at the same time. When we have a dream, it can be tempting to find excuses as to why we shouldn't take a step forward. Rarely are all the details fully known, and all the cons fully analyzed, before we are called to just *go*. As Christians, we can even use the "perfect will of God" as a crutch—that is, a barrier to walking out our destiny.

Thankfully, we serve a faithful God who is with us in all we endeavor. Even if we step out in the wrong direction, He will correct our path. But it's essential to recognize that dreams are in us for a reason. Moving toward those dreams takes faith, willingness to fail, and great courage in the face of the unknown. Nothing worthwhile comes from sitting back and waiting for a dream to happen without action on our part.

God will never leave us or forsake us. He has more in store for us than we could ever ask or imagine!

CHAPTER TEN

IT'S GETTING DARKER

The LORD is my Shepherd [to feed, to guide and to shield me], I shall not want.
² He lets me lie down in green pastures; He leads me beside the still and quiet waters.
³ He refreshes and restores my soul (life);
He leads me in the paths of righteousness for His name's sake.

⁴ Even though I walk through the [sunless] [a]valley of the shadow of death,
I fear no evil, for You are with me;
Your rod [to protect] and Your staff [to guide], they comfort and console me.

—**Psalm 23:1–4**

On July 4, we got up and got the family ready for church, like any other Sunday. When we got there, in our customary manner, we took the older children to kids' church but kept Jude with us for the worship portion of the service since he loved the music so much. He would clap his hands, kick his feet, throw his hands in the air, and sing at the top of his lungs for the entire music set.

It also happened to be Communion Sunday that day. In the middle of the worship experience, each family would come to get the communion elements and then find a place alone to pray and receive the bread and cup together. It occurred to Kenny and me that we hadn't shared the communion experience with Jude before. Since he was so vested in worship, we thought we would take the opportunity to explain the process to him, share communion together, and pray a special spiritual covering over him. In contrast to his dedication, this profound experience was prompted by the Holy Spirit in that moment. Our little boy listened intently, prayed with us, and participated solemnly, as if the moment was just special for him to share with us as it was for us to share with him.

After church, we went home, put Jude down for a nap, and shifted gears to our later Fourth of July activities with Eric and Cindy. While we waited for Jude to get up, the kids played with their friends, and our fourteen-year-old niece visiting from Washington decompressed a bit. At the same time, I made a potato salad for our upcoming cookout.

Before long, Jude woke up. While I tried to force a quick snuggle before we left, I was unsuccessful and wound up handing him over to his daddy. Kenny was on the phone with his mom and dad, so it was perfect for Jude to join in. Kenny wrapped up the conversation with his folks, and we talked about the coming weeks' events—until we realized Jude wasn't in the room.

Almost instantaneously, we both realized the back door was open. Without uttering a word, we began to run toward the door. I blacked out and fell to the ground in panic as Kenny reached the door, and I heard him splash into the spool in the background. He yelled to have me call 911 just as I, in a stupor, rounded the corner and saw him giving Jude CPR. It was almost a complete out-of-body experience as I reached the operator and ran the front door to read the address numbers on the house, because I couldn't remember details as simple as our address.

After getting the address, I turned and immediately went back to Kenny and Jude, praying that I would see Kenny holding my baby wholly revived. When I turned, I quickly glanced upstairs and saw my precious Josiah fighting to come downstairs but being held back by his friend, to protect what he might see. Since I was on the phone and needed to stay until the paramedics arrived, I knew I couldn't run to him at the moment. I desperately needed to stay engaged and do everything I could to ensure Jude would be okay.

Horrifically, when I returned to the backyard while begging the operator to "please make them hurry," I saw Kenny still working on our son. Jude's lips were blue, and he didn't seem to be responding despite Kenny's continued efforts. The paramedics arrived and took over, sending Kenny and me into the house to get us out of the way. We sat on the couch in a daze ... waiting.

After a few minutes, they came through the house with our son on a stretcher and an oxygen mask on his face. Though he was unresponsive, they could get a weak pulse from his femoral artery.

I don't remember a whole lot after that, but I remember Eric and Cindy showing up right as they loaded Jude into the ambulance. Neither Kenny nor I could ride with him, but I would be transported, so Cindy jumped in the back of the police car with me, and Eric stayed with Kenny. Somehow, Trinity, who had been down the street with a friend, and Josiah both wound up in the care of our pastors who lived just a few blocks away.

As Cindy and I got to the hospital, she let me know that Kenny had to stay behind in the house to walk through what had happened with the police and wouldn't be able to join me until later. I don't think I was registering all the activity swirling around Kenny, the kids, and me. In a very short space of time, we each in our individual way had deeply traumatizing experiences surrounding this event. None of us had the presence of mind to think beyond moving from one second to the next, let alone process what was going on with the others in our family. If I hadn't had Cindy with me, I honestly don't know that I could have walked from one place to the next.

Our police escorts brought us into a private room in the hospital, where we sat for what seemed like an eternity. All I could think about was getting to my son. I cared about nothing else, and I desperately wanted to hear them say that he would be okay. A social worker was brought into the room with Cindy and me to ask me a series of questions—the same questions they were asking my husband back at the house. Not understanding that this was protocol, or realizing that the situation called for an investigation, I grew increasingly impatient in my need to know what was going on with Jude.

Finally, a doctor stopped in to let us know that Jude was being admitted to the ICU and that I would be able to go to him as soon as they had him settled. He was alive! A wave of hope hit me. God was going to spare my son—I knew it. He gave us that boy so miraculously; there was no way He would let him be taken from us.

Kenny had gotten to the hospital and was brought to the room with Cindy and me. We didn't have words, so we held each other and cried out to Jesus in sheer desperation. Finally, Jude was settled in his room and we were able to see him.

Before we left that waiting room, though, the doctor stopped to prepare us for what we were about to see.

Jude had not regained consciousness and was being kept alive with life support machinery. No one knew exactly how long he had gone without oxygen, but the next twenty-four to forty-eight hours would determine whether he would survive. There were specific symptoms the medical team was watching for, and warned us about, that would indicate his likelihood of survivability—and, if he did survive, what functions would be impacted long-term.

I don't know how many of their words I really heard. Just knowing he was alive was hope enough for me. As I opened the door of that little room that had been separating us from seeing our son, my friend Tracy was standing on the other side. We knew each other well enough that she knew she was welcome. Yet, the image of her there has burned into my memory in what I have come to believe was a prophetic space in time.

There have been a few such moments on this journey. I don't necessarily know the significance of them all, but what I have learned in trauma is that often, things that seem small can become the very thing we hang onto as truth in our experience of the moment. I'm not sure what I said to her, but I have a clear memory of the thought, *This is going to be a long journey together.* That thought certainly was prophetic. We hugged and prayed for a moment before the six of us went upstairs together.

I don't have a clear memory of walking into Jude's room for the first time. Like that 911 call, many specifics are blank. I do, however, remember the way his vibrant spirit was missing in the room. There were a lot of machine noises and distinctive smells I will never forget. There was also a presence different than what I expected. It was peace without joy, hope with trepidation, and indeed, fear—but not the fear of the enemy. It was more the kind of fear that comes when we ares faced with a situation that leaves us entirely vulnerable and with zero control.

Everything in me felt like Jude would wake up if I could only pick him up and hold him. Unfortunately, he couldn't be moved, and his nerves were so raw from the damage in his brain that any touch caused his little heart to race. In fact, they would have to keep him somewhat sedated just to keep his blood pressure under control while the swelling in his brain was given a chance to subside. We stood around his bed and prayed.

In that critical first twenty-four hours, all of our family began pouring in from Washington. They stood with us as we bathed that room in prayer. We prayed for the staff, the hospital, and of course, surrounding the bed of our son for hours and hours, we begged the God who so graciously gave him to us to give him back. We believed, wept, spoke life in

Scripture, and didn't relent. We weren't about to leave his side.

At one point, I was kissing his face over his bed when he opened his eyes for the first time. I stared back at him and saw a little furrow on his brow. I realized he knew who I was. At that moment, it was as if nobody else was there. I began to tell him how much I loved him, how sorry I was he was hurting, and how much I loved being his mom.

Not knowing how long it would last, I continued looking him deep in the eye for as long as I could keep his attention. I wanted him to know how proud I was that he was mine, that we desperately wanted him well, and that we were so sorry he was hurt. He stayed locked in my eyes as everyone else began to notice his presence. Someone went and got the nurse. When she came in the room, she immediately began to assess him and quickly noticed that he could tell who was talking to him. She then went to the other side of the bed, asking me to follow so we could see if he would turn in my direction. Unfortunately, his gaze didn't follow me, and the moment was over as quickly as it had begun.

Our supernaturally and strategically placed friends Eric and Cindy witnessed the whole encounter. They had enough wisdom to take us aside after things calmed down to make sure we reflected on what had happened. Not knowing what difficult days were ahead, they faithfully obeyed the prompting in their heart to guide us through this specific encounter.

Eric communicated that no matter what the outcome ended up being, we needed to recognize that what had just happened was a gift straight from the heart of God. He had given us a moment with our son, and we would never have to question if he had heard and understood how much he was loved and wanted. Jude knew we were there with him, and I as his mama had the opportunity to say goodbye.

Eric's obedience in sharing what must have been so tricky to talk about was prophetic. About forty-eight hours after the accident, the doctor came to us asking for some privacy. As we sat down with her, I was fully expecting that she would tell us our son was exceptional and, although it is rare to survive such an ordeal, there was hope of a full recovery.

Instead, we listened to her explain how his body was starting to breathe past the machine. He had zero brain function, and recovery wasn't an option. Our Jude wasn't showing any potential of recovery anywhere. In other words, his body could learn to breath on its own (which she felt was unlikely), but if it did, he would have no other brain function beyond that. He wouldn't know he was alive; he wouldn't know who he was. He would simply be bound in a shell, confined to a bed and on machines to keep him fed, as he waited to pass on in two to three years. She felt strongly that the humane choice would be to turn off the life support machines within the next twenty-fou hours. She explained that if we waited longer than that, his passing, though imminent, would be much more difficult.

While I don't have adequate words to describe the emotions that flooded my mind and heart during that conversation, I did feel that the doctor had to be mistaken. She didn't know my son, and she didn't know (that I knew of) the God to whom I belonged. This doctor didn't realize that our family was set apart, special, and exempt from tragedy. I knew my Bible, the Living Word of God that promised safety. I had the answered prayer for Jude's impossible addition to our family, as well as the Passover covering at his birth that solidified the promise that he was born for a purpose. The outcome she assumed just couldn't be the case; she was wrong. I could not wrap my mind around the thought that this could be our story.

Our dear friend Eric always seemed to show up at just the right time. Knowing the difficult conversation we were going to have before it happened, he made sure he met Kenny and me at the door as we returned to Jude's room. He sat us down with words inspired by the one and only true Comforter. He spoke with confidence from the heart of God, yet certainly with a degree of trepidation, knowing how raw we must have been in the moment.

His concern was, first and foremost for our marriage. He had counseled countless couples who had undergone much less than we were about to and not endured. He recalled and shared stories from the Old Testament in which the people of God set up memorial stones to serve as reminders of those times when God intervened, led them, and delivered them. They would position these memorial stones where the encounter took place, and then they would offer a sacrifice. Eric's instruction to us, as we faced the decision the doctor had asked of us, was to set up a memorial stone for our marriage: as we prayed and sought the Lord for direction, we wouldn't look back, question our decision, or blame one another.

Most importantly, we would not move forward until we both were aligned on the decision itself. Our memorial stone was the choice to remember that precise moment in time, knowing that we had prayed, asked the Lord what we should do, and agreed on the answer. We also agreed never to question that decision.

We did just as Eric asked. We prayed, travailed, wept tears of desperation, and got clear direction in our hearts that we were to hold our son before our God with an open hand. That meant shutting off the machines and letting the loving, gracious, miracle-working God who gave him to us choose to heal or take him home.

We got up and stepped into the hallway of the ICU. We asked Eric to get the kids for us so we could tell them about Jude's prognosis and our decision before we talked to anyone else. I can't shake the burning memory of seeing our precious kids in the hospital's waiting room. It was the first time since we all left the house in such trauma. It already felt like we were all changed forever.

We scooped them up, held them for the longest time, and cried and prayed as one, before any words could be spoken. We told them what the doctor said and that we were still praying for a miracle. They were heartbroken but also incredibly brave and trusting in the God they had witnessed answer prayers of their own many times over. The waiting room moment was a memorial stone for us all. We trusted God with the deepest part of our hearts as one, amid both personal heartache and our heartbreak as a family.

As the time came near to act on our decision, the doctor asked how we would like to say goodbye. We asked if we could just crawl in bed with him and hold him. Through these three days, we hadn't been able to pick him up or hold him because his skin was so sensitive to touch. His nerves were all firing at the same time due to the damage to his brain. He'd undergone so much anxiety at one point that he blew a hole in his little lung. He was breathing heavily because noise or touch would cause his heart rate to go through the roof. The doctor was able to oblige our request by giving him a sedative so we could be as near as possible to him.

The hospital took great care to accommodate us as they moved tubes and lowered his bed so we could get on either side of him. We wrapped ourselves around that little boy and prayed a final prayer of desperation. I remember our specific prayer like it was yesterday. We told God that we were choosing to trust His heart and hold our precious boy with an open hand. Still we reminded Him how desperately we wanted this child—how we wanted life to come back into his bones and to share life with him. To all this we added, "Not my will but Yours be done."

We finished praying, and my husband opened his Bible to the book of Jude. He began to read aloud the life-giving Scripture inspired by the breath of God. Jude, as it happens, only has one chapter. Although the doctor told us the process of passing could take as much as twenty-four hours, Jude took his last breath in our arms as Kenny read the last word of the book.

The finality of that outcome was surreal and devastating. We heard what was told to us from the experienced medical team, and we knew the prognosis was grave. Yet, we also had so much faith in the God who gave Jude to us that I couldn't wrap my arms around this reality. We laid there in silence, broken. Neither Kenny nor I was bitter or angry (that would come later), but we hurt from a deep place of disbelief and blind faith. My first thought was, "Okay, God, that's Your decision. I love You, and I trust You."

The nurse came in and confirmed what we knew: Jude was gone, marking the single darkest day of my life. I'll never forget the sense of harsh reality, leaving that hospital room with my lifeless toddler lying on the bed. It felt like such a betrayal to walk away. I can see it in my mind's eye, clear as day: every piece of equipment, every person who could not look us in the eye, the corridor to the rest of our life where we would never be the same. I felt I was abandoning him, like I shouldn't be walking away. That hallway might as well have been a mile long, and it felt like we were moving in slow motion. I held Kenny's hand tight as we went through the door on the other side.

We grabbed our kids and clung to them as our family came around us, consumed by their pain but desiring to comfort us. The twenty-odd friends and family gathered in the waiting room were the community we would need to survive, and we knew it. My husband's young cousin had brought his guitar. As we sat together in that waiting room, unable to move, worship filled our ears. Those gathered with us sang, prayed aloud, and wept with us.

I have no idea how much time passed as we all just sat in the tender presence of God, absorbing the gravity of the moment. We knew that at some point, we would have to leave and try to figure out how to do life. We went through the motions, but all that resonated in my heart was the reality that we would never be the same again.

REFLECTION

God being near to the brokenhearted was a reality I lived but couldn't see in the early days of devastating tragedy. I had come to a place where I thought I would never experience deep pain again. After all, I was a Christ follower. I had been delivered, redeemed, and restored. I expected to live a life of privilege because my life was surrendered to God. But was it?

My expectation with my surrender was ultimate protection and avoidance of trials and trouble. The reality, however, is that we live in a fallen world where we are promised that we will have difficulty to overcome. True surrender for me became trust when I couldn't understand why we weren't spared from what I believe is the worst outcome a parent can face. This pain didn't take God by surprise or take Him off the throne of ultimate control, though. I have learned to trust that He is sovereign and not subject to our expectations. Part of that trust is the belief that His word is true and unchanged, despite what we experience. That word promises a much more fulfilling life in eternity.

What a day that will be!

PART THREE

THE WATER

CHAPTER ELEVEN

FROM THE TEMPLE
TO THE POOL

Even though He kills me, I will hope in Him. Never-
theless, I will argue my ways to His face.

—Job 13:15

The following weeks and months seemed to be a blur. In fact, I don't recall much of the two years following Jude's passing. But despite the unimaginable pain, we were held in an indescribable way. We flew back to Washington and had Jude's remains transported so we could bury him near our roots and our family.

I felt like Naomi in the book of Ruth, entering our little town we had left just a short eleven months before. At that time, we had our little miracle family, dreams in our hearts, and adventure in our sights. Now, we were broken, disillusioned, and in utter despair. Like Naomi, I didn't want to be seen or known as the same as when I left. I was in deep darkness, enveloped by shame because of my ambition and marred by the reality that this was my story. I didn't want this! I had asked for a different story and felt my desire for more had cost my family and me a price I would have never paid, had I only known.

We eventually returned to Vegas while trying to decide if we should pack up and return to Washington for good, tail between our legs. Months had gone by with me in bed most days—screaming, crying, and unable to function. Trying to navigate our life was unbearable, and thank God for my sweet husband. He was able to hold our home together despite my condition. We had moved to a different house across town and tried our best to create some routine for the other kids.

I was navigating a chasm in my heart between me and the loving Father, because of whom I had survived life up to this point. I had learned to rely on Him for every detail. Now, I couldn't speak to Him. I was devastated that He would allow this to be our reality. I loved Him, but I was not okay with Him.

Despite my resistance, He remained near, just as He promised. The sense of grace and mercy in our home was palpable. I remember the first time I uttered a word in prayer while driving to my friend's house. I don't think I said more than two or three words before I was overcome with waves of emotion so encompassing that I had to pull over and sob.

My trust was broken. How on earth could a loving Father allow this outcome? If I could take it on myself, I would never let my children experience such pain. I needed Him to remind me that He had already done this when He sent Jesus. Remembering that would be a long process, but it started with those few words of raw emotion, in which I told Him how hurt I was and let Him bear the burden of my despair. His grace was sufficient in the worst moments. I couldn't see that quite yet, but the process was beginning.

After about four months, I started to get calls from work asking when I would return. I didn't feel equipped to have meaningful conversations with anyone, let alone counsel families about the value of making a memory with their loved ones while they can. The thought of pretending to be normal was daunting enough. Still, I was far too raw to connect emotionally with anyone, especially a stranger.

Then a call came from some dear friends, who asked if I would be willing to become their leader. They were inspired by what success I had found connecting with people before Jude's death and felt that they could help me to find daily purpose. In return, I could help them learn to communicate with people on a deeper level. They assured me that I would not have to pretend when the waves of grief came over me on the hard days. In those moments, I could stay behind the scenes and coach them on what to say when they got stuck or needed to get a sale from a "maybe" to a "yes."

I had told these women that I couldn't possibly return to work in my current state, or likely ever. Yet they were determined to help me understand how I could make a difference for them. I couldn't see past what I thought would be essential for me to contribute in a meaningful way. If I couldn't trust my emotions to stay in check at home, church, or the grocery store, how on earth would I be able to focus on ensuring I had transparent and honest conversations with people about the importance of making memories with their family? I couldn't see that.

Although I might have been too raw in my pain to feel safe sharing my perspective with our guests, I did feel safe with that group of colleagues. They pitched a plan to my company's leadership to offer me a manager role, which would allow me just to coach and guide them until I was ready to interact with the public.

I agreed, and looking back now, I recognize that it was such a loving gift and a humbling reality that I was equipped to help anybody. The God who was in me was light and life to those around me despite how I felt. I simply learned to start taking steps. Fear, depression, overwhelm, purposelessness— whatever I felt, I could not trust it to be the truth. I had to open my heart and choose to believe this deep valley would not be the end of my story. One foot in front of the other. If it wasn't perfect, or if I didn't feel like it, that was okay; it was just important to move.

The movement turned out to be a critical first step. I think of muscles that are atrophied and how painful it is to just start. But when you do, if you keep at it and push through the pain, the healing will come. It's important to remember, however, that breakthrough doesn't come with the first movements. Pushing through the pain often includes feeling like you're not getting anywhere. You'll experience the desire to give up and, without true reflection, the inability to see how far you've come. I honestly could not understand why these wonderful people, who were successful on their own, would want me to lead them in my broken state. I didn't even know how I would lead when I wasn't in a place where I could manage myself. That experience, however, turned out to be an incredible gift and the start of a healing I didn't think was possible.

Going to work every day and being responsible for helping seven staff members earn a living for their families got me back into a routine. It also opened my eyes to a greater calling I hadn't previously recognized: leadership. We had incredible success right away, and I began to find joy in the distraction of having something to do besides think of my pain. I could now give to others, pouring out myself for their success and letting that be the fuel to get me moving every day. It was the beginning of a process I never would have seen coming, but I recognize it today as one of the most pivotal points in this journey—the choice to move.

In the story of the man who was blind from birth, we are shown a man who spent every day of his life begging at the temple gate in Jerusalem. He lived because he asked others for what they had to spare, their "leftovers." As I mentioned at the beginning of the book, when I imagine what his life was like, I wonder if he recognized that the season was different than all others, especially given the extra pilgrims at Passover.

Over his lifetime, he must have heard stories, secrets, and business deals. I imagine he learned about different families, their recollections of the past, and their hopes for the future. He must have heard and been taught about the miraculous exit of his people from slavery into the promised land where he lived. His people expected a coming Messiah who would deliver them again, this time from the oppression of the Roman government. This blind man must have caught wind of the healer from Nazareth before his encounter at the gate.

I even wonder if, in years prior, he had encountered a frantic mother looking for her son. It would have turned out that the boy, Jesus, was so drawn to the temple that He didn't want to leave town with His family when Passover had concluded.

The living this man must have done through others! I can't imagine he thought he had a future even to waste time dreaming about. His future was survival, one day to the next, and that was about it—until one day, he was given a choice.

The choice came on a day that likely started just like any other. Begging at the gate, he heard the words of the disciples, and then the words of the almighty Word made flesh, Jesus.

Jesus was, and still is, the voice of authority. He was the one who had made him, loved him deeply, and longed for him to *see* that he was not broken beyond repair. I believe the healing of this man's sight began when he heard Jesus speak truth and that the chains of lies he wrestled with in his spirit broke at that moment. The Bible doesn't say that, but I know what happens within a heart when it perceives truth directly from the Creator of all things.

Then, when Jesus spit in the dirt, made paste, and put it on this man's eyes, I wonder if he began questioning the truth that had just set him free. Speaking from experience, truth can come into your spirit and immediately set you free, but then begins the work of walking in faith despite how you feel. This man sat in darkness his whole life, hurting and so broken that he didn't dare ask for healing. When his healer made things look darker, the man had a choice to make.

The offensive experience of being spit on or spit at presents us with a choice: remain in your offense or adopt a different perspective. Though he may have felt like he was beyond hope—and even though something offensive was rubbed in his eyes, which likely diminished his ability to see any dim glow of light—he clung to hope and chose to walk in faith.

When you choose to walk in faith and your perspective changes, other things you may have missed tend to come into focus. Jesus not only spit, but He also mixed it with dirt—the substance from which He created man. God's original intention when making man from the dirt was to be in His image and to have a loving, trusting, and fully dependent relationship with Him. Free from sin, mankind was to have a future and hope with Him.

In the exchange recorded in Scripture, we don't hear Jesus address the man directly until the mud was on his eyes. Then He told the blind man to go wash in the pool of Siloam.

That was it? No answers to any questions he might have had? No promise of sight?

The other seemingly offensive part of this story is how far away and difficult the path was to the pool for a man who couldn't see, especially now that spit and dirt blocked out any light at all. The stairs were steep and challenging to navigate for anyone, let alone someone in his condition. Yet he made a choice to move and obey, anyway. That's a choice we all have when we don't get our questions answered. It's a walk of faith on a narrow and often challenging road.

After realizing that I would survive the loss of Jude, I wrestled with sharing his story. Yes, my family's continued existence was evident and, no doubt, a miracle. And I knew that God is a redeeming God who doesn't waste our pain and promises that in the end, *all* things will work together for our good. I have seen that truth come to pass repeatedly over the years, including as evidenced in the history of my life you've been reading. But I couldn't wrap my head around how my son's loss could be redeemed. There was no replacement for him. There never would be; no amount of blessing could cover the devastation, and that remains true today.

But one experience at a time, a faithful, gentle, loving Father began to bring memories to my recollection that would soften that caked-on, dried, and darkness-inducing offense. It didn't happen all at once, though. Each memory was like a splash of water over my covered eyes, letting more and more light creep back in with each splash.

Often, as layers came off, I would experience breakthrough. However, like the blind man, I still had to choose to move through the pain and confusion. Doing so changed my perspective incrementally: as I kept applying the water, I could see progressively more light through the cracks. The trick was, I couldn't stop. I had to continue.

One great example is my memory from the communion experience we had with Jude the day of his accident. The sting of what we believed in our prayers for Jude, with the new reality of what actually transpired just a few hours later, seemed confusing and unbearable. But as I opened my heart, embracing the moment's beauty, that pain eventually turned to gratitude. The reality was, although the Lord gave us a glimpse of truth, we would have to keep applying the water, softening the clay, and breaking through the hardening that came from daily life with offense all over us.

Knowing our hearts as parents, God also knew that we would have questioned frequently if we had prayed over him enough. He even knew I would question the semantics of the "age of accountability" when the enemy tried to invade my thoughts with deception about Jude's security in heaven. God took a painful, confusing memory and continually added clarity. That was where the beauty came through the pain—eventually.

To this day, we still have communion with our kids and our friends, the Jimmersons, every Fourth of July. We choose to remember the beauty of the moment, the gift of the memory, instead of allowing communion to be filled with pain and disillusionment. We rejoice in what the enemy intended to steal from us as we remember the sacrifice of Jesus to be our covering on the anniversary of the worst day of our lives.

Another area where God progressively revealed perspective to me was in that brief but powerful miracle when Jude woke up, on day two of our time in the hospital with him. From the time we faced the shock of his drowning to discovering he was alive, all I had wanted to do was scoop him up, hold him, kiss him, and tell him how loved he was. It was a burning in my heart that remains just as intense today.

Unfortunately, as I mentioned, even a touch would send

his senses into overdrive due to the nerve damage. His heart rate and blood pressure would go through the roof, which was incredibly dangerous. In fact, they intentionally kept him sedated so he would stay calm. It was an awful feeling not to be able to hold him and comfort him in his pain.

When Eric pulled Ken and me aside and reassured us that no matter what we faced next, what we had just experienced with Jude was a gift from God, I was confused and angered. The obedience of Eric in sharing that wisdom would become another washing of the water that softened the hard clay over my eyes, but its healing effects certainly weren't immediate.

In fact, the whole ordeal felt cruel. We were praying with all our hearts for a miracle to heal Jude; we weren't interested in a false sense of hope. The miracle we wanted was to walk out of the hospital with our son. Instead, we got a final good-bye. It was years before I was able to choose to see the moment as a gift. That only came with the constant application of the water of truth, from God's word, that He can be trusted—that He is a good Father and a healer.

In reality, there have been countless stories that the Lord has brought to memory over the years, from the offenses caked on in my childhood to the failures I've experienced and poor choices I've made since. Certainly, stories in this devastating season have continuously washed my heart. As more and more light has come in, the truth that God is present in every second has become a reality more tangible than what I see in the physical.

REFLECTION

Choosing to trust in darkness has to be one of the most vulnerable acts of dependence for someone who can't see. I had perfected the skill of self-reliance and spent a lifetime trying to prove that I wasn't dependent on anyone. Yes, I had developed dependence on God over time. Still, in the early moments of shock and devastation after Jude's passing, my trust was broken in the one to whom I had come to surrender my independence. The depth of shock, pain, and a litany of other emotions regressed into a need to protect myself from more hurt.

Once again, the conscious choice to step out of that self-protection into vulnerability seemed insane. It felt like I was walking blindly out onto a plank over an ocean of fear and uncertainty that threatened to swallow me. I constantly felt that the proverbial rug would be pulled out from under me at any time.

Yet I had to choose to persist in my journey to the pool of God's healing. I knew in my Spirit that the only way to heal was in Jesus. I knew that even though I didn't understand all the reasons why, or how I could ever be normal again, He would be everything I needed if I moved toward Him in blind faith.

Continuing to navigate the uneven steps, the people around me, and the unknown were part of the choice. It was the destination that fueled my determination. I had already experienced the incredible love and freeing power of Jesus to wash away my hurt. I needed that washing again. I'm grateful to have had the opportunity to know what it felt like to find healing that I didn't think was possible.

That remembrance helped me to understand that restoration was still available to me. It gave me the determination to fight for that restoration, the faith to move, and the will to apply the water to my blinded eyes.

CHAPTER TWELVE

THE CHOICE TO SEE

He said to him, "Go, wash in the pool of Siloam" (which is translated, Sent). So, he went away and washed, and came back seeing.

—**John 9:7**

J ust like the blind man in the story, my circumstances gave me a choice: the choice to move, to put one foot in front of the other, in spite of the dirt caked on my eyes. I had the choice to go to the water without the assurance of healing. I could choose to fight through the blindness, down the steep and difficult path to the water. Then I could make the choice to get in the pool and take one splash of water to the eyes after another—and to continue no matter how long it took to break down the hard-packed, sunbaked clay.

It was weeks after Jude's passing before I could utter a syllable in prayer. I remember the first time, in fact, as I mentioned in the previous chapter. Driving to my friend's house silently in my car, all I said was, "Oh, God." Acknowledging Him opened a bottomless pit of sorrow that overtook me so much, I had to pull over and sob for what seemed like hours. I had no other words but "Oh, God," and despair that had become so familiar, I thought it would identify me for the rest of my life. I didn't dare pray again for some time.

My loving Father, determined to reach my heart, gave my husband a hiding place in prayer that I couldn't find. In the mornings, I would join him for a time of prayer and worship, listen to him, and watch him receive restoration from being in the presence of God. I didn't have the strength or ability to say a word for a few years.

Still, I did come and sit, experiencing a sweet presence of indescribable love. Kenny's sweet prayers over me, and tenderness in understanding that the words just wouldn't come for me, spoke volumes about the depth of his character and determination to stand for his family. I fell increasingly in love with the man of God he is, in those moments, and felt safer than I ever had under the strength of his covering.

But the power of those moments wouldn't be realized for years, nor would the gentle truth of the power of moving forward, until I chose to recognize God's presence in all of it. My husband's resolve to do what he could to help me, by simply praying and being unwilling to quit no matter what he saw with his natural eye or how he felt in his own deep pain and suffering, was truly sacrificial. I watched him mourn quietly while trying to be strong so I didn't have to be, day after day.

He had lost his boy, too, his daily work companion. Jude was the one he had been willing to go under the knife again to get. His pain was his choice to move forward in faith, assuring me consistently that had we not been given Jude on earth, we wouldn't have him for all eternity when this short life ends. If that kind of love is not straight from the heart of God, I don't know what would be.

Today, our daily prayer and Bible reading times are profoundly deep and powerful. I desperately need that time of being in God's presence just to exist.

Worship was another area that was complicated to face. Hearing worship was painful, and the thought of singing again was out of the question. I remember one Sunday a few months after we returned to Vegas from Jude's funeral. I thought I was in a place where I could go on time and sit through the worship service. We sang, "Savior, He can move the mountains, my God is mighty to save" on that Sunday, and I was overcome: I had to escape. I grabbed the keys and ran to the car.

Getting in, I locked the door and lay in the back, trying to get as far away from everything as I could, out of sight and out of earshot. I wailed and shouted. I screamed in pain, disappointment, and betrayal.

The worship Jude loved, from the time he would dance in my womb to his expression as a little boy—unashamedly singing as loud as he could, hands in the air and kicking his legs, unable to contain his joy—was a passion we shared. Music, particularly worship, was an expression of the deep and abiding relationship with my Father, demonstrated in beautiful songs that had long been a foundation in my daily walk. I had served in worship for more than half my life, but now I couldn't fathom how I would ever have the ability to connect with God on that level again.

My outpouring of grief was an avalanche of hurt from losing my baby and from loss of trust with the one I had come to abide in, as well as fear that I would never again be able to return to the one thing, worship, that brought me closer than anything else to the presence of God. The wailing arose from the depth of my despair, because my hiding place was gone; the shadow of His wing, where I hid and expressed my love for Him in complete safety, was no more. That felt like more than I could bear.

As church ended and my family got in the car, the familiar sight of swollen eyes and puddles of tears returned looks of understanding pain with no words. I felt catatonic. I was empty even of the effort to hurt anymore; it was no use. I couldn't change what had happened. I couldn't go back, and I couldn't go forward. I felt overwhelmed and completely stuck.

It didn't happen overnight, but the prayers of my husband, family, and friends moved God to keep my heart as soft as possible until a day when our friends Terry and Tracy encouraged me to step forward to lead worship again. By the grace of God, I found the courage to walk onto the stage, even if it meant I would just cry the whole time—and many times, that's precisely what I did. But my stepping out was what made the difference. The willingness to put my pride aside and let people see my pain while making a choice to worship, even when I wasn't feeling it, broke the chains of despair the enemy was trying to place on the gift of God in my life.

The beauty in this was more than the healing that took place in my heart because I made that choice. It was also in the impact I didn't realize it was having on others. God began to reveal to me how much people hurt for all sorts of reasons, and if they could just get hold of the power of worship, the power in declaring the truth of God's love from the depths of their heart in song, strongholds would be broken for them, too.

As my heart opened more and more to hearing God once again, He tenderly offered me more of His perspective on the experiences we encountered along the way. This perspective showed that He had been there with me every step of the way. I began to see where He had carried me and how He had made sure I was loved and cared for by Him, through those people He surrounded me with. With truth, the Lord splashed water over my eyes repeatedly and washed away the evidence of the hurt with each revelation.

In the deep places of my heart, I constantly had Jude's activities and whereabouts on my mind. I wondered who had him. Was he with Jesus directly? Was he scared? Did he miss me? Was he happy? Even though I knew what the Bible said, I couldn't turn off these questions and thoughts.

One Sunday morning, just before we got on stage for worship, God surprised me by speaking clearly to my heart that Jude was always doing what he loved most: making music and worshiping at the feet of Jesus. Picturing him in heaven, engaged in worship, was a revelation deep in my spirit. In this way, God reassured me that even on earth, I have one thing I can do with my son anytime I want. Anytime I'm missing him, I can join him in that worship. This word from the Lord was a significant crack in the hard clay over my eyes.

When you choose to descend the steep and scary steps down to the pool, He will be faithful to strengthen you beyond what you think you are capable of. I didn't think I could get out of bed. I didn't think I could serve my family. I didn't think I would ever again be capable of the essential functions needed to get through life, let alone begin to operate in God's blessings for my life.

But when you open your eyes to see God at work, you will see Him in every detail and in every step you struggle to take. In your moving forward, you'll see Him carrying your pain.

When you open your eyes and look around, and look into the eyes of the people God puts in your path, you will see the comfort that He promises—and it's profound. There is nothing like being broken and vulnerable and opening your heart to fully trust.

And when you recognize that you can trust God—that you are loved, cared for, and protected in times of brokenness—your life can change. Your future can be secure. My movement down the steps gave me the courage to get into the pool, and getting into the pool gave me the courage to apply the water to my eyes. In places of deep pain, we need to move!

REFLECTION

In worship, we sing of the sacrifice of praise all the time. I learned the true meaning of what it was to choose worship, not only when you just don't feel like it, but also when every cell in your body is revolting at the thought that there is anything good in life. It was like breaking through a spiritual barrier of faith. In this, I was fueled purely by my husband's and other loved ones' prayers. Like with other areas of life, worshiping amid my hurt was a conscious choice to believe in the character of God over what I saw in front of me or what I felt emotionally.

Often in life, we have junctures where destiny-altering decisions are made. Crossroads are visible, and we must choose the path to travel. The decision to worship was one of those crossroads for me. Either I was going to believe the whole Bible, *or* I wasn't going to believe any of it. Jesus, as the living, breathing Word of God, was perfectly human and perfectly God. He had to make choices full of faith when nobody in history had experienced anything remotely close to what He would face. Yet He did it, because He trusted the character of the Father.

God has rescued generation after generation who have rejected Him in the most hurtful ways possible. He has provided for the ungrateful, healed the undeserving, and elevated the lowly, only to see them filled with pride and think themselves better than Him. Still, He was willing to offer His own Son's greatest sacrifice for our salvation, healing, and deliverance. Would I have offered Jude to the most deserving of people, full of love and faithfulness? Not in a second. I certainly wouldn't have done so for anyone who would treat his death as nothing more than a nice legend or historical anecdote.

Coming to a place of true worship is found in total surrender—to our expectations, our beliefs, our failures, our disappointments, our dreams, our hopes, and our fears. True worship comes from our recognition that God is not only on the throne when all is right in our lives. It is life-changing to use our audible voice to sing and declare that truth, especially when we don't feel it. Our minds hear what our mouths declare, and our Spirit is refreshed. That's the miracle of the sacrifice.

CHAPTER THIRTEEN

A SETBACK OR ANOTHER LAYER OF MUD?

O my God, in You I [have unwavering] trust [and I rely on You with steadfast confidence],
Do not let me be ashamed or my hope in You be disappointed;
Do not let my enemies triumph over me.

—Psalm 25:2

T he year after we lost our Jude, we underwent another major loss with the betrayal of a twenty-year friendship that layered on unexpected pain and disappointment. In the midst of our grief, we were further plunged into more questions than answers. We were still trying to learn how to move forward from our own losses, and now we found ourselves deeply invested in how to get our bearings back without our biggest support system.

Meanwhile, my sister, who had been diagnosed with breast cancer just before Jude's passing, found her family facing the devastation of divorce after two decades of marriage. This came at the same time she was starting treatment to deal with the cancer.

It felt like wave after wave. We were struck down, one event after the other, but we were not destroyed. Amid everything being thrown at us, beauty began to form on the inside from all the pressure on the outside.

Four months after losing our Jude, I had reluctantly returned to work. I never thought I would learn to function at any kind of normal capacity again, but that handful of amazing women chose to help pull me out of the pit I was in. I believe wholeheartedly that they were sent to encourage me and reveal the gift of leadership in me. I couldn't see myself through all the layers of mud clouding my vision. Their decision to make a difference for me opened doors for all of us professionally, to levels we never would have expected.

God was giving me influence in areas I wouldn't have chosen on my own because I simply did not see the gift He had put inside of me. That season allowed me to begin to see a plan emerge from the dust. The purpose God was revealing in my heart through the experience was about to transform who I would become: the person He had called me to be all along.

My courage to reengage wasn't built on the elements I expected were necessary. Instead, it arose from the motivation of these women who wanted what I had inside. I was learning not to try to perform on my strength alone, but within a community.

These ladies taught me more about how to walk again than I ever could have expected. Although they wanted their own success, I knew they wanted to find a way for me to regain my sense of purpose as well. Their creativity worked both for them and for me, launching a series of continuous successes that paved the way for me to rise professionally, promotion after promotion and milestone after milestone.

Within three years of starting a new career and experiencing waves of pain and loss, I found myself in a vice president role with a large company. I was developing people and running a $100 million business. Ultimately, I was responsible for ensuring that people recognize the importance of spending time with loved ones as the most powerful contribution they can make in shaping their family's future.

Our kids began settling well in school, while our church family became an extension of our tribe. We bonded in a way you can only experience through deep pain and unified purpose. Our friends who pastored the church and met us at the door of that hospital room became our redemption from the loss of our other friends. They were kindred souls sent to be our chosen family forever.

The more God revealed, the more we recognized that we had something to offer despite the pain we carried. My and Kenny's hearts began to turn toward serving others through our hurt. Instead of focusing on our pain, we wanted to give of ourselves—not because we were anything special, but because we saw a need for people around us to know that pain covered by the truth of God's mercy could be redeemed. This understanding allows us to see through hurt into the reality that living in a fallen world doesn't have to define who we are. Jesus does.

We were able to start sharing the truth even when angry, frustrated, and disillusioned. Utter despair did not diminish the power of a loving God who has more for people than they could ever ask or imagine. Life's disappointments don't change that truth!

At the same time, the waves weren't stopping yet. As the months progressed, I got promoted again at work. In a blur, my professional life seemed to be moving forward. My kids continued to do well, by the grace of God. And in August 2011, on the second anniversary of Jude's passing, we went home for a vacation to visit our family.

My sister been undergoing cancer treatments in the early days after our loss of Jude. But within a few months, my sister-in-law, Denna, had also discovered she had breast cancer.

At this point, Denna had been going through a tough fight, including surgery and chemotherapy.

On the trip home, we had decided to go to Portland, Oregon, first, to visit some friends and family. While driving, we got a phone call from Ken's brother, who mentioned that Denna hadn't been feeling well for a few weeks. He decided to take her to the hospital for an X-ray since she had been having severe headaches, and he would call us when they got done.

The follow-up call came while we were still on the road. Ken's brother told us that there appeared to be a spot on Denna's brain. Although we thought her breast cancer was gone, he also said that a lump on her breast had returned, but they had decided not to tell us before now.

Alarmed, we drove into town and went directly to their house. When I laid eyes on my sister-in-law, I was taken aback. She looked sick, frail, and weak, and not the kind of sick you come out of.

As it turned out, a couple of days after we got there, my sweet Denna was flown to Reno to see an oncologist known for success with progressive, late-stage cancer. But since it looked like it had metastasized to her brain, the prognosis wasn't promising. We said goodbye and flew back home within a couple of days to await news of the doctor's plan for treatment.

Unfortunately, the day after getting home, we received a call that Denna had slipped into a coma. All the family was encouraged to go to Reno to say their goodbyes. Here we were again, at another crossroads—another opportunity to beg God for healing of one of our own. We asked in desperation, but God chose to take her home within a few short hours of our arrival.

This beautiful woman of God, with two teenage girls, who had been a wife to my brother-in-law for over twenty years, was gone. She had been part of my life since I was a teenager myself, and was one of the main reasons I found my husband. There was the immediate shock and sadness, of course, but also a tinge of jealousy that she was with my son, whom I desperately missed.

When we said goodbye to her in that room, it felt like it was, indeed, the end of me. I couldn't handle another loss. We went from the loss of our own child to the loss of our friends and now the loss of our sister. Denna was my kids' auntie and the mama to the nieces we loved so much. I didn't want to see my children hurt anymore. They'd lost their two aunties: first, their godmother, who had been part of their life from birth, had been our friend; now, the auntie who had lived next door to them when they were growing up in Washington. It was too much for all of us—too much heaviness and too much devastation. I wondered how we would ever get back up with hope and live with joy.

Despite my constant feeling of brokenness, God slowly continued to call me into a place of worship. I stepped out in obedience, not because I felt it but because I knew I needed to continue stepping toward Him instead of allowing my emotions to drive me away. That decision was pivotal.

When I agreed to lead a team of worship leaders full-time as the director, I made a conscious decision to serve out of my desperate need to draw closer to the Lord. I needed to understand His heart in allowing so much to come against us when we served Him to the best of our ability. The truth that "His strength is perfect" when ours is gone, as the Steven Curtis Chapman song goes, became how I lived life. I had to live if I were going to survive all this.

That step would ultimately wash away more dirt than I could have realized at the time. My choice was conscious, but my movement felt numb and empty. Then, one day, I realized that the choice to move toward God, especially when I didn't feel it, was teaching me more about the power of trust than I expected. In addition, I learned the power in making a sacrifice when you feel least capable.

REFLECTION

Opening our eyes and developing focus happens after we choose to apply the water. However, if heat has dried the caked-on mud obscuring our vision into clay, the layers will not come off with a quick, one-time application. The water must be applied repeatedly and allowed to penetrate the hard crust. I would go so far as to say that fully committing to the experience by immersing yourself in the pool with abandon is even more effective.

Of course, that's not in the biblical story, but I know the feeling of sheer desperation that drives complete surrender. That desperation can be found at the core of many people who have felt entirely out of options but discover one last hope. That hope resonates with their spirit and breathes life into their soul. I wholeheartedly believe that the man blind from birth was driven to the pool by a "last hope" desperation that helped him overcome every obstacle along the way.

It must have been the most profound experience for this blind man to get to the pool. But what about his experience when he started applying the water in obedience? How often did he apply water before the crust started to soften and light began peering through the cracks? We don't know for sure, but I know from my experience that nothing happens overnight. Faith and hope will drive the action, but trust builds in the practice of obedience. The act following the decision to believe is what truly ignites the faith journey.

Consider what it must have been like for that man once the mud started to soften and come off. He wouldn't have known if he was seeing or not; he would only know that there was light where darkness had been. Then, I imagine, he would have started to see outlines of images and colors that he wouldn't know how to describe. Likely, this exhilarated him and sparked more determination to keep applying the water. Having never seen before, he would have to figure out what he was looking at. Yet he knew he was seeing something.

The message for us is to stay in the pool, continuing to apply the water of God's word as we allow faith to grow and healing to take root. It will not be instant; it will not even be comfortable all the time. In fact, we should expect to grow quite weary in the process—but there *will* be breakthrough and healing. Just don't stop.

CHAPTER FOURTEEN

OUT OF THE FIRE BUT NOT SMELLING OF SMOKE

And the LORD will continually guide you,
And satisfy your soul in scorched and dry places,
And give strength to your bones;
And you will be like a watered garden,
And like a spring of water whose waters do not fail.

—Isaiah 58:11

Not long after that, I was offered a promotion. The job was in Hawaii, which seemed like a perfect, fresh start for our family. It would be a real opportunity for us to close the chapter on Vegas and all of the years of crushing upon crushing we'd experienced. My career was a place of security and refuge for me. I could go to work and focus on making the business successful while forgetting the deep pain that lingered inside. So we packed our belongings, grabbed our kids, and moved over to the island of Maui.

In Maui, I began to experience a different kind of crushing, on the professional side. Despite my pain, I'd had such wild success over the previous few years that I didn't know what to do when the work got really hard. I had to battle the thought in my mind that my career would fail as my parenting had. Yep—that was a root running deep. I had failed as a daughter when I ran away, as a sister when mine didn't want me, as a Christian when I didn't live a life reflecting Christ.... I could go on and on. The narrative went deep, and I believed it down in my soul.

I didn't know how to handle this feeling of impending doom and ultimate failure. I was convinced that the subsequent loss would be my career. However, I had an entire team of people looking to me for direction and inspiration, so I could never let them see the crack in my confidence. I had to figure out how to hold my head high and fake my way through the war inside of me to have a fighting chance of making them successful. It was exhausting to pretend I was okay, and I felt like a fraud as I encouraged others to give their all when I felt so defeated inside. I had no choice, though, but to move forward.

I was in a fight for my life and didn't think I could possibly make it through. I never experienced being suicidal, thankfully, but I certainly thought life as I knew it was over. God had turned His back on me. Every element of our life was under attack, and for whatever reason, I just knew we were sunk.

As I recall the feelings I wrestled with, I can't help but think again about the man who was blind from birth (I really should invent a name for him, one of these days!). I imagine him walking down the steps to the pool of Siloam, through crowds of people who likely bumped into him without a thought. Maybe they knocked him over, not realizing that his already blind eyes were caked with mud. Think of the willpower it must have taken him just to keep going, wondering if he would ever reach the pool! He must have wondered how he would get in and if, in the end, washing his eyes with the water would do anything for him at all.

I love the stories in the Bible when you're reading about devastating circumstances and then you get to the "but God" part. We were about to have such a moment, as the opportunity to move back to the mainland opened up. A series of events led me to surrender completely.

When my assignment on the mainland became clear, it was to a place the family ultimately didn't want to live. I couldn't ask them to sacrifice any more than they already had for my sake. Kenny and I decided that I would resign from my leadership role with the company and walk away. We had simply been through too much.

That place of surrender opened a door for me with another company. The offer came within days of our decision to leave my previous job. It was nothing short of miraculous! This other company hadn't been on my radar, nor would I have had the strength or fortitude to go after the job if I had known about it. I didn't end up having to sacrifice my career, after all. Rather, I now had a great opportunity for further growth tossed into my lap, in a place my family was excited about settling down in: San Diego.

The Lord graciously held our hands through the selling of our home in Hawaii, which would have been a massive financial burden had He not intervened. That move initiatted a wonderful season of rest and recovery.

Even now, as I'm telling you this, I don't know how our story ends. I know that God is a redeemer, but I can't begin to fathom how He would redeem the loss of Jude until we join him in heaven one day. Then, I imagine I will see redemption at every turn.

I know the pain of great loss, and I know how confusion can overwhelm us in the heaping of disappointment and piling on of more loss. But I also know that God is faithful and His word is true. He is with us in every moment, in every circumstance, and in every disappointment, in the most profound ways.

God is "man enough" to tolerate our anger with Him, our confusion, and our frustration with Him in those places of pain. In fact, I've never felt more loved than in those days when I would scream from the deepest place in my gut. I felt safe in His love even when being honest about my questioning. I was authentic, and He was listening with compassion. Even as I would pour out my heart to my God in anger and pain, He was not angry with me. He could handle it. Those ended up being the moments that opened the door for healing.

Though healing my heart completely will take a lifetime, I know the day will come when I will feel the weight of my son in my arms again. For now, with all confidence, I know that the Lord will also carry you in your darkest times. Our God is a healer, a redeemer, a perfect Father, and the finisher of our faith.

The most critical place you will find yourself in deep pain is at the crossroads of choice: the choice to believe, the choice to see, and the choice to move forward. That may mean a baby step or a shift to the right or left. The key is to move, and to move toward Him. Prayer is the perfect place to start.

Often, we think of prayer as a formal session in which we make requests and hope we say things in a way that encourages God to give us our way. It's actually so much more than that. For many months, I had such a hard time saying even a few words to the Lord. I was not feeling okay with Him, because I couldn't believe what He had allowed to transpire. My trust (or my expectation) was broken. Yet I still had security in knowing that despite what I saw right in front of me,

His word remained true. He loved me at a depth I couldn't comprehend.

And as I've shared already, when I couldn't find the words, my husband could. He was able to pour out his heart before God in a way I could not. When I heard his prayers over me, I was amazed at his ability to communicate so openly God, whom I loved but was really angry at. Sometimes movement is just putting yourself in a place where you can receive ministry. Placing myself in the atmosphere my husband created, and allowing him to minister to me with his prayers, was precisely where the Holy Spirit could break through, layer by layer.

That first step toward the pool for that blind man was probably the hardest, as was mine. Movement builds momentum, and your courage will grow into more steps until eventually, you have the courage to step into the water.

As I opened my heart more and more, I started to see God's hand at work in and through me. It was faint at first, like that first splash of water over caked-on mud. But the more I tried to see Him, the more light came through. Then, as I applied more water, my vision gradually got clearer. Even in my anger and disappointment, I knew He was there, and I knew He wasn't going anywhere.

In fact, the more I applied healing water to my eyes, the more He stirred my heart with a resolve not to let my life be about pain, my career, or me. Instead, my life should reflect the truth of His promises and goodness—even in the darkest places.

The real tragedy would have been for me to give up and allow all that deep pain to be wasted. I'm here to tell you that the more you move toward Him, even in the tiniest way, the more He will make up the distance and give you new vision. That new vision won't be impaired by years of offenses, disappointment, and pain. He will *never* leave you or forsake you. Even when you can't see Him, feel Him, or recognize His presence, He is there with you.

For me, another big step was to start moving toward ministry, specifically in the intimate and deeply personal place of worship, as I shared earlier. Making a conscious choice to serve in the area of my greatest need was a big move, but God met me in there in such a profound way. I wonder what He is leading you to step into, service-wise? The Bible says to seek first His kingdom, and I can't think of any better way to step out in faith than to be His hands and feet for someone else who is hurting.

Worship was where I connected with God. It was a vulnerable step of renewed trust that was necessary but also incredibly difficult.

What is that place of vulnerability where you connect with God in the deep cavern of your heart? Is it loving on kids? Is it speaking words of life to the lonely and discouraged? Whatever it is for you, take a step.

The more I made a choice to obey the leading of the Holy Spirit and apply the water of worship again, the more profound my intimacy with the Father grew, and so did my trust in Him. In fact, one Sunday morning, in gentle whispers in my heart, He said to me that in my willingness to step out in worship, I was actually doing the same thing Jude was doing; we were, in essence, doing it together. After all, Jude's life in heaven is all about worship! When I miss my son or when I'm longing for a memory of him, all I need to do is worship, too.

I took a step, and God came running toward me with revelation only a caring and trustworthy Father would bring. As I took steps forward, God He allow me to see more and more where He had been all along.

Another time, in my despair, I was hurting in a way only a mother who'd had her toddler ripped from her could. My arms were empty. I couldn't feel his weight anymore in my arms or in my bed, whether at night or in the morning when he would crawl in and hog all the space. He used to fall asleep and get crazy hot, making me want to get away from him just to cool down. I didn't get to have that feeling anymore, and I missed it desperately. At times, I even wrestled with the question of Jude being in heaven.

Additionally, he was a toddler, utterly reliant on his parents, especially his mom. I struggled with his whereabouts and wondered if he was fearful. Did he understand what had happened? Did he miss me? I had begun reading a book called

Heaven by Randy Alcorn, because I was searching desperately for understanding of what life was like for Jude. I had never thought of heaven so much before in my life. It was a place we were going to go someday. Our eternity was secure, and we would live forever instead of burning in hell with the devil. Great. Awesome. But I had never had an investment there as I did now, and I wanted to know more.

Randomly, one day, I got a call from a friend in Washington who wanted to check in and see how I was doing. She shared with me that she had just read a book about a little boy who had gone to heaven. I hadn't read many such stories, because I knew my heart was vulnerable. I chose to stick with Scripture, wanting to ensure I didn't acquire a wrong mindset from well-meaning people who weren't biblically sound. (Note that even the mention of a boy who went to heaven and returned was really hard for me to hear.) I couldn't wrap my head around why some kids get healed and stay on earth while others have to go too soon.

My friend was compelled to share, though, so I listened. She shared about how this little boy's mom had some miscarriages and that in his vision, he saw a place where all the babies were. I wondered about the relevance to me until she said it was a place where many people loved to come care for and see the babies. Then she said, "It's funny. What made me want to call you is, the little boy communicated very clearly that the babies were all very happy, they were well, and though content, still missed their mommies."

Again, like the gentle voice of the Lord, this was a reminder that as Jude was experiencing the bliss of heaven, he had a perspective that I didn't. He had comfort in knowing that his mommy would join him soon. Mommy wasn't forgotten, and she was going to be okay. That was the gentle nudge and message of the Lord: Jude's mommy was not forgotten.

Had I not been taking steps to open the door for the Lord to speak, I would have missed that extraordinary and intimate acknowledgment of my questions. God was not validating the story, nor was He slapping me on the wrist for having those questions. He simply loved me by acknowledging that He heard the questions deep in my heart that I hadn't spoken to anyone. Moving toward Him, washing with the water of His word, clears up our ability to notice when He is simply saying, "I love you through someone else."

I could continue to share story after story of moments when God has redeemed me by giving me perspective. The memories that would be bitter have become sweet with the recognition of His grace and the ability to see clearly.

Several times in the early days after Jude's passing, random people would talk to me about the book of Ruth. I would get furious and frustrated at first when they would approach me with their well-intentioned words of encouragement. All I could think about in Ruth was a woman the Lord rescued from the loss of her husband. Everything came back to her. She had this perfect little story of redemption and healing tied up in a proverbial bow, with a new husband and a child who would be in the lineage of Christ. It's truly a wonderful story.

The part I didn't catch until years down the road, though, was that the Lord sent those people to remind me of that book, not because of Ruth but because of Naomi. Unlike Ruth, Naomi didn't get a new husband. She didn't get her boys back. She did, however, get to hold the promise of a future. She got an opportunity to witness the miracle of life coming from the ashes of her tragedy.

Naomi saw the redemptive heart of God in Boaz, for Ruth, and in Obed, Ruth's son, for her. When we are able to see things from God's perspective, versus the limited view of our offense, we see the miraculous way God turns all things for good. Naomi was the grandmother of Obed, who was the grandfather of David, in the lineage of the ultimate redeemer for all mankind—Jesus.

I can't help but believe that the parts we don't know about Naomi as her life progressed include the many redeeming moments God gave her as He danced over her and poured out His love on her life. I'm confident He loved her and guided her forward with an anointing for enduring her pain as she trusted Him with the deepest part of her heart.

That's the hope I have for you in reading this book. I don't have a big revelation about why God allowed this to be my story. However, I have a future and hope in a promise that I will be with my son again for all eternity. I, too, will be held tight as I live a life fulfilled by Christ and seek Him first while on this earth. There is no way to make sense of a deep and abiding joy when your heart has been broken, but that is a fulfillment God promises when we choose to trust Him.

Though sharing my story has been in my heart for a while, I've wrestled with writing this book. I've wrestled, mainly, with the fact that I don't have a beautiful ending that seems complete, like in Naomi's story when Ruth handed her that sweet baby boy. I hear countless stories of women who have lost children and gone on to have other children. The great testimonies of how they felt like their child was redeemed in those future children are lovely and inspiring. But I don't have that, nor do I think that another baby could ever replace the hole left by losing a child. (I don't think other women feel that way, either). In fact, I will have a gaping hole in my heart until the day I am with Jude again. The hole, however, has some blood-stained stitches holding it closed and keeping it from taking on infection.

I will always miss my son and carry the weight of that pain, but I will also rejoice in the beauty of the gift of him. After all, you can dance with a limp—you just learn to dance a little differently and weave that limp into the pattern of your expression in worship.

I have seen a side of our God that few experience without going through hardship. Still, I find myself amazed at His grace. On the other side of hurt is the view of a loving Father who is forever merciful and understanding of our humanity, and who is a safe place where we can go to heal. Many times over the years, when running from Him and from my pain, He was faithful to guide me lovingly back to Himself. I know a side of Him that is redeeming in ways I would have never expected.

I also know that He is purposeful in everything, and I'm confident that He still has a blessing and a dream beyond my wildest imagination waiting for me. I know it like I know He's real, and I know it for you, too. Whatever pain you're experiencing, whatever crushing you have endured, I can assure you that there is joy to come in the morning. It is joy you can't explain; people will look at in you and wonder how on earth it is possible. But God will, without a doubt, redeem your pain. It's who He is. It's in His nature.

To be sure, you will have to take some steps forward in faith, down the steep staircase from the temple gate to the pool. You may feel alone in that journey. You may feel incapable of making the trek. You might even be angry that there's dirt covering your eyes. Just remember that dirt clouds our ability to see clearly; that's why it takes faith to move forward. I know He will be there with you in your slightest movement. I know He is drawing you to that pool for healing. I know He wants to wash that dirt off, layer by layer, with the water of His word. Redeeming is His nature—He can't help it!

Plus, He desperately loves you and wants to see you receive victory. He wants to show you how He has been there all along and to whisper reminders of grace in your ear as you gain strength. He can be trusted! So be blessed, be encouraged, and know that you are in the palm of His hand.

REFLECTION

I find it significant that I'm writing this final passage on the anniversary of Jude's trip to heaven. The days leading up to this particular moment every year face me with the choice, all over again, not to get stuck. Though my body responds with weakness and my countenance with sadness, if I didn't choose continuously to apply the water even now, I know that I would be vulnerable to the attacks of the enemy on my healing.

Resilience is found by continuously doing the things that have brought you the victory to begin with. It's found in the remembrance of who God has proven He is, time and again, despite the emotions that threaten to swallow you up. Healing is a continual process of trust, obedience, and inexplicable faith.

Resilience is also found in sharing your heart. You, by reading this book and allowing me to share my story, overcome the enemy. I encourage you to be willing to share your journey with someone else as well. There is power in community, and victory awaits on the other side of seeing someone else refreshed and renewed in hope because of what you have overcome.

> And they overcame and conquered him because of the blood of the Lamb and because of the word of their testimony, for they did not love their life and renounce their faith even when faced with death.
>
> **—Revelation 12:11**

ABOUT THE AUTHOR

T rina Miller is a business executive, wife, mother, sister, and friend. Most of all, Trina is a Christ follower who purposes to live out her passion of inspiring others toward deeper levels of trust in the Lord by overcoming life's biggest struggles.

A survivor by nature, Trina shares how each stage of her life presented a choice either to lean in and press through or to make excuses and tap out. Trina's book is meant to inspire faith and trust in a God who is always in control, always for you, and always working for your good.

Made in the USA
Las Vegas, NV
22 January 2024

84734079R00108